THE
HOLY LAND
IN THE TIME OF JESUS

There are a number of HORIZON CARAVEL BOOKS
published each year. Titles now available are:

THE HOLY LAND IN THE TIME OF JESUS   MARCO POLO'S ADVENTURES IN CHINA
THE SPANISH ARMADA   SHAKESPEARE'S ENGLAND
BUILDING THE SUEZ CANAL   CAPTAIN COOK AND THE SOUTH PACIFIC
MOUNTAIN CONQUEST   THE SEARCH FOR EARLY MAN
PHARAOHS OF EGYPT   JOAN OF ARC
LEONARDO DA VINCI   EXPLORATION OF AFRICA
THE FRENCH REVOLUTION   NELSON AND THE AGE OF FIGHTING SAIL
CORTES AND THE AZTEC CONQUEST   ALEXANDER THE GREAT
CAESAR   RUSSIA UNDER THE CZARS
THE UNIVERSE OF GALILEO AND NEWTON   HEROES OF POLAR EXPLORATION
THE VIKINGS   KNIGHTS OF THE CRUSADES

American Heritage also publishes AMERICAN HERITAGE JUNIOR LIBRARY
books, a similar series on American history. The titles now available are:

GEORGE WASHINGTON AND THE MAKING OF A NATION   WESTWARD ON THE OREGON TRAIL
CAPTAINS OF INDUSTRY   THE FRENCH AND INDIAN WARS
CARRIER WAR IN THE PACIFIC   GREAT DAYS OF THE CIRCUS
JAMESTOWN: FIRST ENGLISH COLONY   STEAMBOATS ON THE MISSISSIPPI
AMERICANS IN SPACE   COWBOYS AND CATTLE COUNTRY
ABRAHAM LINCOLN IN PEACE AND WAR   TEXAS AND THE WAR WITH MEXICO
AIR WAR AGAINST HITLER'S GERMANY   THE PILGRIMS AND PLYMOUTH COLONY
IRONCLADS OF THE CIVIL WAR   THE CALIFORNIA GOLD RUSH
THE ERIE CANAL   PIRATES OF THE SPANISH MAIN
THE MANY WORLDS OF BENJAMIN FRANKLIN   TRAPPERS AND MOUNTAIN MEN
COMMODORE PERRY IN JAPAN   MEN OF SCIENCE AND INVENTION
THE BATTLE OF GETTYSBURG   NAVAL BATTLES AND HEROES
ANDREW JACKSON, SOLDIER AND STATESMAN   THOMAS JEFFERSON AND HIS WORLD
ADVENTURES IN THE WILDERNESS   DISCOVERERS OF THE NEW WORLD
LEXINGTON, CONCORD AND BUNKER HILL   RAILROADS IN THE DAYS OF STEAM
CLIPPER SHIPS AND CAPTAINS   INDIANS OF THE PLAINS
D-DAY, THE INVASION OF EUROPE   THE STORY OF YANKEE WHALING

A HORIZON CARAVEL BOOK

THE
HOLY LAND
IN THE TIME OF JESUS

By the Editors of
HORIZON MAGAZINE

Author
NORMAN KOTKER

Consultant
FREDERICK C. GRANT, D. D., TH. D.
Professor Emeritus of Biblical Theology
Union Theological Seminary

Published by American Heritage Publishing Co., Inc.
Book Trade and Institutional Distribution by
Harper & Row

FIRST EDITION
Library of Congress Catalogue Card Number: 67–12487
© 1967 by American Heritage Publishing Co., Inc., 551 Fifth Avenue, New York, New
York, 10017. All rights reserved under Berne and Pan-American Copyright Conventions.
Trademark CARAVEL registered United States Patent Office

FOREWORD

In the twelfth year of Emperor Tiberius' reign, a new Roman procurator was sent to the eastern Mediterranean to govern the subject land of Judaea. Some ten years later he was removed from office for a misdeed and exiled to Gaul, where he may have committed suicide. The man, Pontius Pilate, could never have imagined that his name would be forever fixed in history through a minor event of those years in Judaea—his sentencing to death of an accused rebel, a Jew named Jesus.

The Holy Land, as Judaea, or Palestine, came to be known, was the scene of great political, social, and religious upheaval in the two centuries surrounding the life of Jesus. The Romans under Pompey arrived as conquerors in 63 B.C. Not until A.D. 135, two centuries later, was Roman mastery of the troublesome Jewish homeland made complete. The Jews, inheritors and guardians of an ancient belief in a single, all-powerful God, were dispersed to many lands. But from this trial—and from the cruel persecutions of subsequent generations—emerged a stronger Jewish faith.

The followers of Jesus, originally a minor sect within Judaism, eventually forged a powerful religion out of the belief that he was the Christ, or Messiah. As different as they remain, Judaism and Christianity share a common reverence for the Old Testament and for the Holy Land, where Jesus once walked, and where, since 1948, the dynamic new Jewish state of Israel has flourished.

The story of a land in ferment and of the growth of these two faiths forms an absorbing and important historical chronicle. It is a tale richly illustrated by the work of talented, devout artists of many lands and many centuries. Present-day photographs show the rugged, dramatic Holy Land, as changing and changeless now as it was in the time of Jesus.

THE EDITORS

Jesus presides over a wheel-pattern map of the world in the thirteenth-century Latin psalter illumination opposite. The known world radiates out from Jerusalem (center) and is surrounded by a narrow outer band of ocean.

RIGHT: *A twelfth-century illumination traces Jesus' family tree. From Jesse, bottom, spring King David, Mary, and Jesus (top).*

BIBLIOTHÈQUE DE DOUAI: GIRAUDON

COVER: *The four Evangelists, Matthew, Mark, Luke, and John —holding their texts—appear in a Coptic (Egyptian Christian) codex.*

SMITHSONIAN INSTITUTION, FREER GALLERY OF ART,
WASHINGTON, D.C.

FRONT ENDSHEET: *In a painting from Dura-Europos, Syria, Aaron stands before the Temple. Sacrificial animals are at the sides.*

NATIONAL MUSEUM, DAMASCUS:
GOODENOUGH, *Jewish Symbols in the Greco-Roman Period:*
COURTESY BOLLINGEN FOUNDATION

TITLE PAGE: *An early symbol for Jesus was a fish. The initials of "Jesus Christ, Son of God, Saviour" spell* ichthys, *fish in Greek.*

LOUVRE

BACK ENDSHEET: *In a Russian church screen of the sixteenth century, Jesus, with angels, sits between Mary and John the Baptist.*

WALTERS ART GALLERY

BACK COVER: *A tablet with the Ten Commandments in Hebrew illustrates a page from a rare fourteenth-century German manuscript.*

COURTESY OF FRANK J. DARMSTAEDTER,
JEWISH THEOLOGICAL SEMINARY OF AMERICA

CONTENTS

FOREWORD 6

I A KINGDOM FOR HEROD 10

II FAITH OF THE JEWS 26

III VOICES IN THE WILDERNESS 42

IV JESUS OF NAZARETH 56

V PAUL, THE FIRST CHRISTIAN 84

VI JERUSALEM BESIEGED 110

VII STRUGGLE TO SURVIVE 130

ACKNOWLEDGMENTS 150

FURTHER READING 151

INDEX 152

Ous auons moustre
au uolume de dauant
cestuy a la mort de la
royne alexandre. Or
racomptons les choses qui sensuiuet
et ne tendons a nulle autre chose fors

a riens trespasser des choses qui ont
este faictes en puruoiant ala memo
yre de ceulx qui les liront. Car a
ceulx qui escripuant hystoures ou ra
comptent choses anciennes il conui
ent pour lancennete mettre ou faire

I

A KINGDOM FOR HEROD

In the first century B.C. Rome gained control of the Mediterranean world. Her invincible legions had marched across parts of three continents, conquering kingdom after kingdom and plundering venerable cities that had been rich and powerful when Rome herself was still a cluster of hill settlements. Rome's enemy Carthage, the proud maritime city on the North African coast, had been leveled to the ground and salt strewn over its soil so that nothing would ever grow there again. Athens, in Greece, and the great Egyptian temple-cities beside the Nile had seen the Roman troops parade by, their javelins and their eagle standards held high and the feathers on their crested helmets waving in the wind. Roman legionaries had traveled as far as Britain to the north, and to the east as far as the edge of the great desert that separates the lands bordering the Mediterranean Sea from the rest of Asia.

The armies of Rome subjugated farmers and city dwellers and wandering tribesmen; they gathered beautiful works of art from Greek cities and shipped them home to adorn the luxurious villas of Roman aristocrats; and everywhere they went, they requisitioned gold and stripped the temples of treasures.

But wherever the legionaries went, they established order and the rule of Roman law. Where before there had been squabbling city-states, constantly at war with one another, princes murdering their brothers to gain thrones, petty monarchs vying for a few square miles of land, pirates terrorizing the sea lanes, and highwaymen robbing travelers, there was now peace and safety.

Most of the conquered nations accepted Roman rule.

A proud legionary with a crested helmet decorates a Roman mosaic.

In the fifteenth-century manuscript illustration opposite, by Jean Fouquet, Pompey's troops slaughter Jewish defenders as they enter Jerusalem's Temple. The French court-artist created a medieval decor for the ancient shrine.

The conquerors taxed their subjects heavily, but once tax money was collected, they usually respected local customs and local traditions. Roman generals even offered sacrifices to honor the local gods and often entertained the population with gladiatorial games and circuses. Roman governors erected aqueducts to bring water to the cities and built highways to foster travel and trade. Under Roman protection, the Mediterranean world grew prosperous.

In at least one part of their empire, however, the Romans found themselves hated. That was in the land that came to be known as Palestine, at the eastern end of the Mediterranean Sea. Its four regions, Idumaea, Judaea, Samaria, Galilee—stacked from south to north like boxes one on top of another—were conquered in 63 B.C. by the Roman general Pompey. The conquerors allowed Palestine's rulers to exercise limited power as long as they promised to enforce peace and remain loyal to Rome. It was not easy to maintain peace and loyalty, however, for the population of Palestine was divided. In Judaea and Galilee the people were mostly Jews, who fiercely upheld their ancient religion and refused to mingle with other men, men who worshiped idols instead of a single, invisible God. They found it intolerable that Roman law should take precedence over the laws of the Torah—the first five books of the Bible—which they believed had been given to them by God Himself.

In Idumaea and Samaria, however, the population welcomed the Romans. The Idumaeans were forced converts to Judaism, and the Samaritans were a racially mixed people who observed part of the Jewish religion. The two peoples saw no reason to hold themselves apart from the rest of the world. They believed that the unification of the shores of the Mediterranean under Roman rule brought prosperity, and they were anxious to share in it.

But most of the Jews refused to cooperate with the Romans. They were determined to maintain their own identity and not be swallowed up in the vast and expanding imperial power of Rome. They knew they could do this only by remaining apart and by following their own traditions. For two centuries (63 B.C. to A.D. 135) conflict raged between the Romans and the Jews, sometimes breaking into open warfare but more often seething under the

Pompey the Great

The map opposite, encompassing the area between the Dead Sea and Damascus, shows many Old and New Testament sites famous in the time of Jesus.

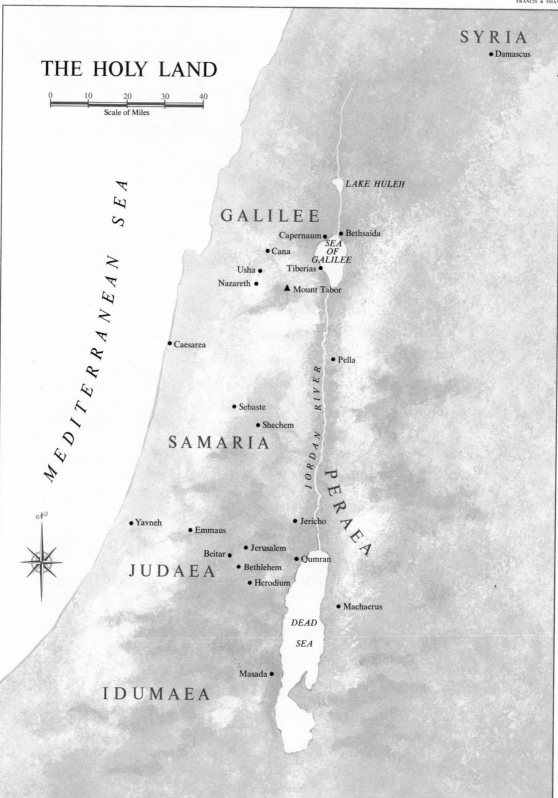

THE HOLY LAND

0   10   20   30   40
Scale of Miles

SYRIA
• Damascus

MEDITERRANEAN SEA

LAKE HULEH

GALILEE

Capernaum •   • Bethsaida
• Cana   SEA
        OF
        GALILEE
Usha •   Tiberias •
Nazareth •   ▲ Mount Tabor

• Caesarea

• Pella

• Sebaste
• Shechem

SAMARIA

JORDAN RIVER

PERAEA

• Yavneh   • Emmaus   • Jericho
Beitar •   • Jerusalem
• Bethlehem   • Qumran
• Herodium

JUDAEA

• Machaerus

DEAD
SEA

Masada •

IDUMAEA

surface. Whenever war broke out, the Jews eventually lost, but they were never really defeated. Indeed, the great conflict that the Romans thought they won had unexpected consequences. It made the Jewish religion over into a newly strengthened faith capable of surviving for centuries in the future, wherever the Jews might wander in a hostile world. It also fostered the birth of another religion—Christianity —which began as a tiny sect within Judaism but which was eventually adopted by the entire Roman Empire and spread to the ends of the earth.

The Romans of the time could not foresee these developments, of course. All they knew was that the Jews stubbornly insisted on holding to their own ways. And so, in order to encourage integration of the Jews into the empire, the rulers Marc Antony and Octavian, some twenty years after Pompey's conquest, decided to place a puppet king on the throne of Judaea—a ruler who would support the interests of Rome and firmly suppress any attempts by the Jews to assert their independence.

Rome's candidate for the throne was a young man named Herod. He was a tall and handsome Idumaean prince just under thirty years of age, an athlete, a hunter, and an accomplished military leader whose talents might be put to use to protect the eastern borders of the empire. Herod had many other qualifications to recommend him to Rome. Since his family had been converted to Judaism, the Jews presumably would not object to him on religious grounds. Skillful in handling men, ruthless when necessary, and kind when kindness seemed to be the most practical course to follow, Herod had the potential to be a strong ruler. He could be charming and shrewd, for he was well educated and had learned the polished Greek manners that were required for leadership in the ancient world. Herod had made himself a close friend of some of the most powerful men in Rome; in addition he had valuable connections in the Arab lands that bordered Palestine. Rome needed friends there in order to maintain trade, and there Herod could be very useful. He had grown up in Petra, the immensely wealthy desert capital that controlled the caravan route that reached from Arabia to the Mediterranean

Petra's treasury façade (opposite) is seen through a rift in the sandstone cliffs that for centuries provided the city with natural defensive walls. Secure and wealthy, the city enjoyed the benefits of both Greek and Roman culture. Above, on stone, is a fragment of the Greek word for "theatre."

The head of the young Roman consul Octavian is capped with the corona civica, *or oak-leaf crown.*

shores, and he was related through his mother to its most important and richest citizens. Herod's father, Antipater, had also found favor with the Romans. He had served as governor of Idumaea, winning for his sons Herod and Phasael the governorships of Galilee and Judaea. To Antony and Octavian, all this seemed to provide Herod with a powerful claim to the royal palace that loomed high above Jerusalem, the capital and holy city of the Jews.

But there were several drawbacks to Herod's candidacy —and they were serious ones. He had no legitimate right to succeed to the throne of the Jews. He was not related by blood to the Hasmonaean dynasty that had been ruling over the Jews for more than a century. He was not even of Jewish blood at all. And the Jews, over whom he longed to rule, hated him fiercely.

Herod had won the admiration of the Romans when, as governor of Galilee, he had put down a minor rebellion in 47 B.C. The rocky hills of his province had been infested with rebels hiding out from the government in inaccessible caves. To Herod and the Romans these men were brigands, interested only in robbery and in avoiding payment of taxes to the foreigners who controlled the country. But in their own eyes they were patriots who were resisting foreign domination. They operated on the borders between Syria and Galilee and were supported by the Jews of the region but feared by the Syrians. In a province under his control, Herod could not tolerate their presence and their harassment of government troops. He gathered a small force of soldiers and swiftly marched against them, climbing to their hideouts in the hills to root them out. He killed a number of rebels in pitched battle. Many of the rest he captured and promptly put to death.

Herod's triumph pleased the Romans immensely, but in Jerusalem there was a different response. Herod had put down rebels with whom many Jews were in sympathy. And he had also broken the law by executing men without a trial. To the Jews this was a crime worse than rebellion. Many of them frowned upon capital punishment, preferring to let a prisoner escape rather than punish an innocent man. Since Herod had scoffed at this tradition, the relatives of the slain men prevailed upon the aged ruler, or ethnarch, of the Jews, Hyrcanus, to call him to account. Even though the Jews were under Roman domination, they still maintained their own courts and their own limited forms of government under the Hasmonaeans.

Herod reluctantly rode south to Jerusalem to stand

trial. To bolster his defense, he took along a bodyguard —and a letter from the Roman governor of Syria warning Hyrcanus that Rome would retaliate if Herod was harmed. The trial took place before the Sanhedrin, an assembly of seventy elders, which, along with the ethnarch, constituted the highest governing body of the Jewish religion. Most accused men who came before the tribunal walked in wearing a black robe of mourning, unshaven and with their hair unkempt, in an attempt to move the court to compassion. Herod was too proud for that. Accompanied by his soldiers, he marched into the great stone hall where the Sanhedrin sat, ranged in a semicircle, and stood before them dressed in a robe of purple, the color of royalty.

Sixty-nine of the seventy members of the Sanhedrin who tried him—aristocrats, priests, and learned rabbis— were too intimidated to do anything but vote for acquittal. Only one rabbi, Shemaiah, dared to take a stand. He got up and berated Herod for coming before the court in so insolent a manner, and he rebuked Hyrcanus and his fellow members for being so terrified of the soldiers and of Roman power that they put up with Herod's behavior. And he warned the ethnarch and the assembly that when Herod himself had enough power, he would never treat them as gently as they were now treating him. His fiery prediction was to come true, for when Herod did finally seize control of Jerusalem, years later, he put to death all of the surviving members of the court that had dared to place him on trial. Only one life was spared—that of Shemaiah himself, because Herod admired his courage.

Under Roman protection, Herod slowly increased his power. But in the year 40 B.C. his career, and Roman domination of Palestine, were threatened by an invasion of the Parthians, conquerors of Persia, the only people powerful enough to challenge Rome at that time. In their wake came Hyrcanus' nephew Antigonus, eager to seize the throne for himself. The Parthians cared little who held the throne of Judaea, but they did want to see the Romans expelled from Palestine and from the entire eastern Mediterranean region. Antigonus had to offer a tempting bribe to get the Parthians to help him: a sizable sum of silver and, as a special bonus, five hundred aristocratic women of Jerusalem. The Parthian commander could add the women to his harem or sell them into slavery if he preferred. One Parthian general found the offer too tempting to turn down. He promised Antigonus his help and ordered his soldiers to march south along the fertile coastal plain

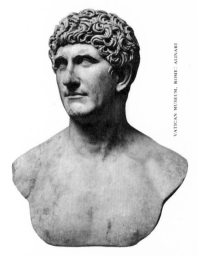

Marc Antony, co-consul with Octavian, ruled the Roman provinces in the eastern Mediterranean area.

of Palestine toward Jerusalem. Antigonus' own army also headed south, along a more difficult route inland, marching up and down the hills that cross Galilee and Samaria.

Along his way Antigonus enlisted a great many Jews to fight under his standard. Many joined because they feared that Herod might be the next king of Judaea, and they preferred to live under Antigonus, who was a legitimate Hasmonaean heir to the throne. They also preferred to live under the control of the Parthians, who might prove to be gentler masters than the Romans.

In Jerusalem, Herod waited with his brother Phasael, governor of Judaea. The Romans had promised help, but it was slow in coming. Phasael, who attempted to negotiate with Antigonus and the Parthians, was imprisoned and later either took his own life or was killed. When he heard of Phasael's capture, Herod realized he could not withstand both armies. Deciding that his only chance lay in escape, he collected his wife, his mother, and the five hundred terrified women and sent them out of Jerusalem, on donkey-back, in the middle of the night, hoping they would elude the enemy. Herod and his troops followed the fleeing women, staying in the rear to fight off pursuers, as they headed south through the barren hills of Judaea to seek refuge in the wilderness fort of Masada near the Dead Sea.

There, on an isolated mountaintop accessible only by narrow paths that could easily be defended against a whole army by a few soldiers, Herod was safe. One dizzying trail that led to it was called the Serpent. It was so narrow and twisting that a man climbing it had to place one foot directly ahead of the other in order to avoid falling into the deep gorge beneath. One false step would topple him to his death. The fortress, located in one of the most inhospitable landscapes in the world, overlooked the Dead Sea, which, at 1,291 feet below sea level, is the lowest point on earth. The desert surrounding the fort was only rock and sand, but the flat summit of Masada boasted a few acres of soil that could be tilled. Cisterns cut into its rock stored whatever rain fell in that arid land. If it rained even a few days a year, a besieged group might hold out indefinitely.

Herod, however, had little intention of spending his days sitting quietly on a mountaintop until the Romans

Excavators at Masada unearthed the storage jars and cooking pots above. The sandals, skull, and braids of a Judaean woman (below) were also found buried at the site.

The recently excavated site of the Masada fort is seen in the aerial photograph opposite. Rectangular storerooms cover a large area of the plateau (at top). The walls and terraces below are the ruins of Herod's palace.

sent an expedition to rescue him. He decided to go off in search of aid himself. Leaving another brother, Joseph, in charge at Masada, Herod went first to Petra, where he was denied entrance, and then to Egypt, where he got no assistance from Queen Cleopatra. Rome, he finally came to realize, was his only hope, and at Alexandria, he set sail for Italy. He landed at the port of Brundisium on the heel of the Italian peninsula, and from there he traveled on horseback directly to Rome. As soon as he arrived in the city, Herod went to the house of Marc Antony.

Antony was horrified at the story of calamity that Herod unfolded to him. He took Herod to Octavian, and once again the Idumaean prince told his tale. The two men, who together ruled the Roman world, were determined to save Herod, name him king of the Jews, and restore him to power in Judaea. Herod was led through the streets of the city to the Forum and conducted to the great hall where the Senate had convened, waiting to welcome him. Senator after senator rose up to praise him and to point out the advantages his rule could bring to Rome. His bravery and the help he had given to Rome were applauded, and his military skills were described enthusiastically. By acclamation, the senators proclaimed him king of the Jews.

With Marc Antony and Octavian on either side of him, Herod then marched in triumph across the Roman Forum, followed by the consuls of Rome and by the senators in their flowing togas. The solemn procession passed along the Sacred Way, going by the huge market building and the Temple of Saturn, where the enormous Roman treasure was kept, and then climbed the steep path up the Capitoline Hill overlooking the Forum. The party reached the Temple of Jupiter and entered its gates. There, before the altar of the pagan god, they performed a sacrifice to celebrate the naming of Herod as king and prayed to Jupiter for good fortune in all the years of his reign. An ox was sacrificed, and wine was poured out before the altar. Then they went to the house of Marc Antony to celebrate the inauguration of Herod's reign with a banquet.

There was in Rome a sizable number of Jews who lived in their own neighborhoods, with their own synagogues, or meeting places, and their own shops. Herod's behavior

Columns of the Temple of Saturn (at left, foreground) are the sole remains of the great edifice that Herod passed on his way to the Capitoline Hill. Beyond lie the ruins of the Roman Forum, hub of ancient Rome.

scandalized them. It was bad enough that an unpopular king was being imposed on their homeland; what was really unforgivable was that he had celebrated his accession to the throne with a pagan sacrifice, thus breaking the commandment to worship only one God, the commandment that distinguished the Jews from the rest of the world. Herod had begun his rule as the king of the Jews by flouting the most sacred belief of his own subjects, a belief for which thousands of them had died.

In Judaea itself, the Jews felt the same way. Herod had been made king by foreigners for the benefit of Rome and not of Judaea, and in the very act of inaugurating his reign, he had betrayed his people. Although he had been named king, his kingdom was not yet in his power, and there were many among the Jews who were determined to see that it never would be. Herod was well aware of this enmity, and he did not linger in Rome. He hurried back to Palestine, for the title of king was almost all he possessed. He would still have to fight hard and long—for the next two and a half years, in fact—to gain his kingdom.

As soon as Herod reached Palestine, in 39 B.C., he recruited a Jewish army loyal to him. Supported by Roman troops already at his disposal, he marched to Masada to relieve his relatives, who were still besieged there. As his army headed south, Herod subdued the towns and villages along the way. But at every spot where rocks and caves could afford cover to an enemy, his men were ambushed by the soldiers of Antigonus, who was now ruling in Jerusalem. Despite constant harassment, they reached Masada and raised the siege.

Before he could take Jerusalem, his most important goal, Herod had to subdue the rest of the Holy Land. In the countryside of Galilee he met with strong opposition from Jewish rebels who were able to hide out for months against an invading army in the many caves concealed among the hills. On one mountainside a rebel band had found refuge in hideouts so remote that it seemed as though they could never be reached. The mouths of their caves overlooked the only path by which they could be approached, for the mountain above them was so steep that no man could climb down it. Any soldier who tried to pick his way up the mountainside to attack the caves was an easy target for the rebel marksmen.

In order to drive out the rebels, Herod tried a daring stratagem. He built several wooden cages and enclosed his most dauntless soldiers inside them. The cages were at-

A Roman relief depicts priestesses offering a sacrifice at the altar of Vesta, goddess of the hearth.

tached by iron chains to enormous pulleys on top of the mountain. Then they were carefully lowered down over the precipice until each was directly opposite the entrance to a cave. The cages were so well constructed that it was easy to shoot out of them, but the most skillful rebel marksman found it almost impossible to shoot into them.

Herod's soldiers, armed with long iron hooks, reached into some of the caves and swept out their occupants, knocking them over the side of the mountain onto the sharp rocks below. Some of the rebels were smoked out when fires were lit at the entrances to their caves; others were killed in battle by the soldiers who swarmed out of their mid-air cages and into the depths of the caves. Others surrendered to Herod, asking only that he spare their lives. Still others jumped to their death rather than be captured and sold into slavery.

In the year 37 B.C., after he had pacified the rest of the country, Herod made his final assault on Jerusalem. It was, literally, an uphill fight all the way. He began at the town of Jericho, one of the oldest-known cities in the world, which lies eight hundred feet below sea level, near the shores of the Dead Sea. To reach Jerusalem, his troops had to go only forty miles, but the last twenty of those miles meant a rugged climb of 3,300 feet along a winding and

Caves like those in which rebels hid from Herod's soldiers dot a hill in the Galilean countryside.

NORMAN KOTKER

Herod, wearing his crown and holding a scepter, leads his army past defeated Jews into Jerusalem. Fouquet's fanciful illustration places King Herod in an elaborate Temple containing a purification font and a sacrificial altar.

difficult road through a wilderness landscape so wild and so empty that it resembles the surface of the moon. Although Herod was opposed by nearly six thousand men under Antigonus, his army managed to force its way into the uplands after a pitched battle. Reaching the hill country north of Jerusalem, after burning the villages of his opponents along the way, Herod cut the road to the north to prevent reinforcements from reaching Jerusalem. With Antigonus' main army out of the way, only the walls of Jerusalem stood between Herod and complete control of the country.

But the walls of Jerusalem were strong; it took two and a half months of siege before Herod was able to get past them. Roman battering rams were brought into use, but even these could not shake the walls of the city. The defenders sneaked out at night to burn the siege engines, and whenever the Romans started to build new ones, the Jews, braving ambush, darted out from the safety of the city walls and burned those too. Among the Roman legionaries supporting Herod were sappers, men who dug tunnels beneath the walls in order to weaken them. The Jews within the city also built tunnels. When they encountered the enemy sappers, they fought them in underground skirmishes, forcing the Romans to flee. Finally, however, a scaling party of twenty picked men succeeded in climbing the walls, and they were soon followed by others. After weeks of siege, the outer walls were taken. But the besieged army continued to hold out, for the city was defended by the inner walls as well. It took weeks more before Herod's army could get past the second walls.

The catapult, a siege weapon that was perfected by the Romans, flung huge projectiles hundreds of yards.

When the attackers finally broke through, there was fierce hand-to-hand fighting in the narrow streets. The Roman troops were bitter after the long hard siege, and they began to burn, kill, and pillage so savagely that Herod begged the Roman commander to call them off. What good would it do, he asked the Roman general, to empty the city of both men and money and leave him king of a desert? He accompanied this question with a sizable bribe for the general, along with gold for each of his soldiers, and managed to convince them to restrain themselves. It had cost Herod almost all of his money to capture the city. Although his capital was turned into a shambles after two and a half months of siege, he had finally gained control of his entire kingdom. And the Jews, twenty-six years after Rome had first conquered their land, now had a king imposed on them by their conquerors.

FAITH OF THE JEWS

Herod's hold on the land he had seized by conquest was precarious. The Romans would be happy with him as long as he maintained the peace, but he was still considered a foreigner and an intruder by the Jews. In order to win them over, he decided, shortly after he gained control of Judaea in 37 B.C., to rebuild the ancient Temple that crowned the heights of Jerusalem. The Temple was the focus of the Jewish religion and the place to which every Jew was supposed to come as a pilgrim three times each year.

The original Temple had been built by King Solomon, almost a thousand years earlier. It had centralized the nation's worship at Jerusalem and had been a place where the scattered Hebrew tribes could put aside rivalry and come together in peace. That building, whose beauty was legendary, had stood for four hundred years. It was destroyed in 586 B.C. by the Babylonians when they conquered Jerusalem and carried a great many of the Jews into exile. Later, when the Jews returned from Babylon, the Temple was rebuilt, but not on a scale to equal Solomon's sanctuary. In fact, when it was rededicated late in the sixth century B.C., the old men who remembered how beautiful Solomon's Temple had been wept at the dedication ceremony instead of rejoicing.

Herod was determined to give the Jews cause for rejoicing, but when he proposed to their religious leaders the building of a new and grander Temple, his offer was greeted with suspicion. Many of them mistrusted him so much they imagined that he was secretly planning to tear down the ancient sanctuary, on the pretext of rebuilding

As God hovers over Israelite slaves, Moses pleads before Egypt's Pharaoh in the illustration opposite from the Psalter of Saint Louis, a thirteenth-century manuscript. Above, left, is a fifth-century mosaic lion of Judah.

it, and put up a pagan shrine in its place. In order to convince them that he had no such intentions, Herod was forced to spend years quarrying enough stone to reconstruct the entire Temple before he was allowed to tear down any part of the old structure. He collected a thousand wagons to carry the white stone from its quarry near Jerusalem, and he hired ten thousand carpenters, masons, and stonecutters to work on the outer structure. To build the Holy of Holies, the innermost sanctuary, which only the High Priest could enter, Herod selected and trained one thousand priests. At last he was given permission to start demolishing the old structure, and at the beginning of the year 19 B.C. actual construction was started. Although some of the work proceeded quite rapidly, the Temple in Jerusalem was still unfinished at the time of Herod's death fifteen years later.

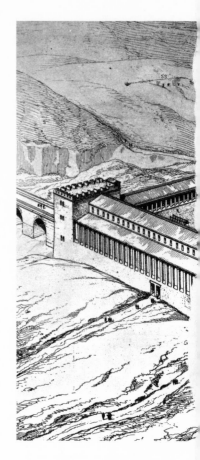

The new Temple taking shape followed closely the specifications of Solomon's Temple. But, because Herod had a passion for grandeur, the courtyard that surrounded the building was much larger and more ornate than the one Solomon had built. When the Temple was finally finished, the vast enclosure covered thirty-five acres, about one sixth of the total area of the walled city of Jerusalem. Building it was a complex engineering job. To extend the pavement, Herod had to level hilly areas and fill in depressions and even carry some of the Temple courtyard upon arches over a valley that cut through Jerusalem.

The entire enclosure was paved with colored stones and surrounded by a colonnade of white marble columns, each of them almost forty feet high. This was what came to be called the Court of the Gentiles, where anyone could enter. Strollers gathered there to gossip and to shelter themselves from the sun under one of the archways. Passers-by could be seen taking short cuts through the Temple court from one side of Jerusalem to the other. Country people entered bringing sheep to be sacrificed to God as atonement for transgressions; women came—as was the custom—to offer sacrifices of doves or pigeons after giving birth to children. There, the devout came with offerings of grain or spices or simply to pray in the Temple or study in the synagogue that stood in the great court. Many Jews from abroad could be seen, for by now there were hundreds of thousands of Jews who had left Palestine to live elsewhere. To buy animals for sacrifice, these people exchanged—with moneychangers who transacted their business in the courtyard—foreign coins for the special currency that was used

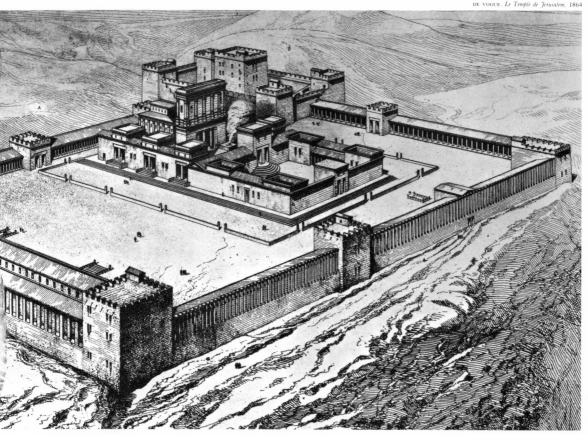

The nineteenth-century drawing above is considered the most accurate reconstruction of Jerusalem's Temple site. The enormous Court of the Gentiles surrounds the two smaller courts of the inner building complex. The first, the women's court, leads to the entry gate of the priests' court and the altar. This court contains the Temple building itself. The cluster of large buildings at the far end of the outer court is the Antonia fortress. Scholars disagree on the building's appearance. The model at left suggests another style.

29

in the Temple. There, too, came the flower-decorated carts containing the first fruits of the harvest season, which the country people sent to the Temple each year as a thank offering to God. Laden with barley and wheat, olives, figs, grapes, and pomegranates, the carts were usually accompanied along the first stages of the journey to Jerusalem by throngs of farmers singing psalms.

The completed Temple and its priesthood were famous for their lavish display. The flaxen-colored veil hanging in front of the Holy of Holies was embroidered in blue, scar-

NATIONAL MUSEUM, DAMASCUS: GOODENOUGH, *Jewish Symbols in the Greco-Roman Period*; COURTESY BOLLINGEN FOUNDATION

A third-century wall painting from the ruins of the synagogue at Dura-Europos in Syria symbolizes the collapse of paganism before the sacred Ark of the Covenant containing the Jewish law. At the right of the Ark are two broken idols taken from their pedestals in the shrine behind them.

let, and purple. The colors had their own mystical symbolism: flax for the earth; blue for the sky; scarlet for fire; purple for the sea. The dress prescribed for the High Priest who entered into this most sacred sanctuary was a rich outer robe of blue that reached almost to the floor. From the fringe of the garment hung golden bells and pomegranates: the bells possibly symbolizing thunder; the fruit, lightning. An embroidered belt, which repeated the colors of the veil at the door, held the garment together. Above was a breastplate containing twelve jewels—one for each of the twelve Hebrew tribes. On his head the High Priest wore a linen miter tied with a blue ribbon and surmounted by a golden crown. On the crown appeared four Hebrew consonants—the equivalent of YHWH—standing for the sacred name of God, Yahweh, which could not be written out in full or spoken aloud.

The inner courts of the Temple were especially holy. No gentiles were allowed to enter them. Upon the walls of these courts a sign in both Greek and Latin threatened death to trespassers. One of the courts was used mostly by women; beyond was a second that was open only to male Jews. Within it was the Temple building itself and the great stone altar that only priests were allowed to approach. It was an enormous rock—as big as a house—that can still be seen in Jerusalem today. There, at the altar, the actual sacrifices took place. Some were official, presented by the whole Jewish nation. Every morning and every evening, while the piercing sound of a silver trumpet rang out over Jerusalem, a white lamb with no blemishes was slaughtered and then burned. Other sacrifices were offered by King Herod or were paid for by a Roman general who might be kindly disposed toward the Jews and their religion. But most were the offerings of the people, and during each day, as animal after animal had its throat cut, the scene in front of the altar often came to resemble a busy slaughterhouse.

In this, the Temple of the Jews was like the temples at which pagan gods were worshiped. In their cults, pagans also followed a detailed ritual in which an animal or a food or drink offering was minutely prescribed and the order of sacrifice was carefully observed to keep from displeasing the god to whom the offering was made. It was like the practices in the temples of Babylonia, to the east, where the fierce gods could be appeased only if the complicated rituals of sacrifice were followed exactly. Jewish sacrifices also resembled those of Greece and Rome, where the pious

The widespread use of ritual objects in the ancient world is suggested by this Syrian votive offering, which has characteristics of both Roman and Egyptian gods.

The holy Ark and the ritual implements of the Temple decorate this sixth-century mosaic from the Beth Alpha synagogue in Israel. Menorahs (seven-branched candelabra) and lions symbolizing the tribe of Judah stand on either side of the Ark. On the left is a shofar, *the ram's horn sounded during ceremonies at the Temple, still used in synagogues on certain holy days.*

offered sheep and oxen at the temples of many gods. The Greeks and the Romans also poured offerings of wine and oil at the shrines of departed heroes or dead ancestors—and sometimes even offered gifts of milk to the snakes that were kept in many households by the superstitious who believed that they gave protection. In a small way the ritual even resembled the customs of Egypt, where each day the strange idols of the gods, shaped like jackals or hawks or hippopotamuses or cats, were unveiled and "awakened" by the priest. The images were offered food and flowers and anointed with oil, and once or twice a week they even had their clothes changed.

But in one way, a most important way, the Temple differed radically from pagan temples. The difference was so great that Jews of antiquity were looked on as a race different from all others, a race that separated itself from all other men and thus was often treated with contempt. For in the innermost sanctuary of their Temple, where other nations would have enshrined the images of their gods, made of gold or marble or silver or wood, the Jews had absolutely nothing. Their God was invisible, and they were forbidden by their law to try to depict Him. Their God was, they believed, the only God who ever existed, the Creator of all the universe and of all mankind. He was so vast and so powerful that no man could ever fully understand Him,

The journey of Jacob, grandson of Abraham, and his family to Egypt is illustrated by Meir Yaffe in this fifteenth-century German Haggada. These books prescribe the ritual for the domestic service on Passover eve and are often richly illuminated. Haggadoth are never carried into the synagogue, where strict rules against imagery prevail.

much less represent Him. Other nations worshiped many gods, each of whom watched over a particular aspect of life and none of whom was powerful enough to rule alone. The Jews' concept of one all-powerful God was so difficult for foreigners to grasp that they often accused the Jews of atheism—of denying the existence of divine beings altogether—and they hated and persecuted them for it.

The Jews' worship of one God, and their scorn for idolaters, was ancient. According to tradition, their religion had been founded long before the time of Herod, when their ancestor Abraham—who probably lived between 2,000 and 1,750 B.C.—destroyed the idols worshiped in his father's household in Mesopotamia and left the country between the Tigris and Euphrates rivers. Abraham migrated to Palestine where he could freely worship one God. It is unlikely that anyone will ever know whether Abraham was a historic person or a legendary hero. In any case, nomadic shepherd tribes, the Israelites, or Hebrews, claimed descent from Abraham and worshiped only his God. Driven by famine from their new homeland, many of

Another of Yaffe's Haggada illustrations depicts Pharaoh and his queen watching as a servant drowns the male infants of the Hebrews.

these people entered Egypt some time in the seventeenth century B.C., when that country was under the control of Semitic tribesmen related to the Hebrews. When Egypt threw off the control of the Semites, the Hebrews were enslaved, and they remained in bondage in Egypt for generations. Early in the thirteenth century B.C., however, they freed themselves and fled from Egypt.

During their subsequent wanderings in the desert separating Egypt and Palestine, the Jews originated their unique religious code. On Mount Sinai, God Himself, they believed, had delivered to their leader Moses an extensive set of laws whose most famous section is the Ten Commandments. Jews were forbidden to kill, steal, lie, or be envious. They were taught to observe the Sabbath as a day of rest, to protect the poor and the weak, to be kind to animals. These laws brought a powerful religious ideal to the world, for they firmly declared that any offense one man committed against another man was a sin against God.

In time the wanderers joined with other Hebrew tribes, descendants of Abraham who had not been in Egypt, to form a confederation, the Twelve Tribes of Israel. Some time around the twelfth century B.C., the Israelites, by then a nation sworn to follow the law of Moses and fiercely devoted to the worship of only one God, migrated into Palestine and slowly gained control of the hill country that rose on both sides of the Jordan River.

By the year 1,000 B.C., they were a powerful kingdom ruling a wide territory under the warrior King David and his son Solomon, as renowned for his wisdom as his father had been for his military skill. But the Israelites' power did not last long. The nation that David had attempted to unify by making its central city, Jerusalem, the capital, split in two. The kingdom of Israel had its capital at Shechem; and Judah, in the south, kept Jerusalem as its capital. Each half was an easy prey to the powerful empires that soon arose nearby. The Assyrians came, conquered the northern half, Israel, and eventually destroyed it by exiling many of its inhabitants and resettling foreigners among those who remained. Their mixed descendants, the Samaritans of Herod's time, were not considered to be true Jews.

The southern kingdom of Judah lasted longer, but eventually it too was destroyed, by the Babylonians in 586 B.C. Many of its people were also sent into exile.

In addition to these hostages, many other Jews eventually left their small and overcrowded homeland. This emigration came to be known as the Diaspora, or dispersion. By the time of Herod, considerable numbers of these voluntary expatriates lived in their own communities in Arabia, Egypt, Greece, and even in Rome itself. But wherever they settled, Jews remained true to their unique religious beliefs.

During the Babylonian captivity, the exiled Jews maintained their separate identity. The priests and scribes among them believed that the banishment from Palestine was an expression of God's displeasure. Hoping to find the reason for God's dissatisfaction, they began to study more closely the laws and rituals that formed the basis for their

The 7,497-foot-high north peak of the Gebel Musa range in Egypt's Sinai Peninsula is traditionally regarded as Moses' Mount Sinai.

religion and to write about them. They gathered together their tales of the creation of the world by God, His designation of the Hebrews as His Chosen People, and their subsequent history—from Abraham through the period of wandering in the desert. These stories, along with the ethical code of Moses and lengthy descriptions of the rituals to be performed in the worship of God, made up the Torah—or the first five books of the Old Testament: Genesis, Exodus, Leviticus, Numbers, and Deuteronomy. In later years, in Babylon and following their return to Palestine, the Jews added other writings to their holy book—additional historical narratives such as the books of Joshua, Judges, Samuel, and Kings; psalms and proverbs; and the writings of teachers and prophets such as Isaiah, Jeremiah, Ezekiel, and Micah. The enormous work, comprising thirty-nine books, was probably completed about the fourth century B.C. However, it was only officially adopted in the form recognized today in the first century A.D.

Encircled by flames, Moses (above) displays the law to the Hebrews in a thirteenth-century Haggada. Two scenes from the Dura-Europos frescoes (right) show Moses leading the Exodus and then closing the Red Sea on the pursuing Egyptians.

Thus, with the political power of the exiled Israelites eliminated, their religious zeal increased. The justice and morality of the laws of Moses came to be stressed more and more, and ritual—with the Temple at Jerusalem destroyed —became less important. The words of the prophet Isaiah, "I hate and despise your sacrifices," now had added meaning for the Jews. God would not accept sacrifices for their own sake, Isaiah had taught; the man who offered them had to be good. Another prophet, Micah, had summed up all of the laws of the Torah in one sentence: ". . . what does the Lord require of you but to do justice, and to love kindness, and to walk humbly with your God?"

Some fifty years after their defeat of the Jews, the Babylonians were in turn conquered by the Persians, and the exiled Israelites were released from captivity. Many of them returned to their homeland and about 538 B.C. began rebuilding the Temple in Jerusalem. The new Persian masters of Palestine allowed the Jews a good deal of religious

freedom, but the Greeks, who arrived in the fourth century, were not so generous. After nearly four hundred years of foreign domination, the Jews rose in revolt against their oppressors in the year 167 B.C. Led by Judas Maccabee, a shining figure in Jewish history, the people of Palestine rid their land of foreigners and re-established the Jewish monarchy under the rule of his family, the Hasmonaeans. This dynasty ruled the Jews as kings and high priests until the advent of Herod.

A remarkably strong and durable religion—one with enormous power to withstand suppression and even gain new power from persecution—had developed from all these centuries of wandering, conquest, and exile. But the Temple, and the priests who controlled the form of worship there, no longer played a dominant role in the nation's religious life. Their importance, in fact, had been eclipsed by that of the scribes. These men were teachers who had collected together the Old Testament books of the Bible and had taught them to the people during their years of trial. Herod, however, failed to appreciate this transformation of the religion. Thus, when he rebuilt the Temple, thinking he would be loved by the Jews as much as the builder of the first Temple, Solomon, had been, Herod was deceiving himself. The Temple was important to the Jews, but not all important. For now, along with the Temple in Jerusalem, there were in the villages and towns synagogues where the people came to study the Torah and hear the laws and history of their ancestors read to them. The scribes lived in close touch with the people, while the priests of the Jerusalem Temple did not. The scribes found that certain of the ancient laws had to be adjusted to meet the times they lived in or the demands of daily life; the priests and their followers were determined to maintain the teaching of the past unchanged.

Moreover, by the time of Herod, the nation was fiercely

A seventh-century stone sketching records a famous legend from the Babylonian captivity: Daniel in the lions' den. Cast before the beasts to face certain death, the Judaean noble was saved when God sealed the mouths of the animals.

The Maccabees (right) battle for control of Judaea with the Seleucidae, the ruling Greek dynasty. In this thirteenth-century manuscript the foes are armored knights.

divided into two rival groups. The great mass of the people supported the Pharisees, followers of the scribes who had taught and interpreted the law to the people during the preceding centuries. The most fervent among them joined in groups to study and observe the law and to avoid contact with those Jews who were not as devoted as they and who were thus considered impure. In their observance of Judaism, the Pharisees were extremely zealous. The most devout lived in separate villages and refused to recognize Herod's or anyone else's right to be king, for they believed that only God was king of the Jews. The Pharisees refused to eat from a dish that had been used by an "impure" person or consume food that had come from a supply not taxed by the Temple. And yet, even though the Pharisees followed every detail of the law, they were, particularly under the great leader Hillel, concerned with far more than just the letter of the law. Some of Hillel's precepts are echoed in the later Christian teachings. "What is unpleasant to yourself do not do to your neighbor," he declared, "this is the whole law, all else is only commentary." Hillel also admonished his followers to "judge not your neighbor until you are in his place."

The Pharisees insisted that the animals sacrificed daily at the Temple be paid for by the taxes of the whole population and not from contributions by the wealthy. This was to remind the populace that the Temple belonged to the entire nation and not to Herod or the rich people only. They introduced universal education to the country and insisted—sometimes without success—that all children learn how to read. They were the most faithful followers of the law, but they also allowed a good deal of freedom in interpreting it. They allowed poor people to marry without having to pay the customary bride-purchase price, and they insisted on simple funerals so that the rich could not put the poor to shame, even in death.

The Pharisees scorned the Greek civilization that Herod encouraged in the country, and they were shocked when he built a hippodrome for chariot racing in Jerusalem and an amphitheatre outside the city walls where men fought with wild beasts and with one another in gladiatorial combats.

Yet, the Pharisees in general supported a policy of uneasy cooperation with foreigners in their land when it did not interfere with the practice of their religion. However, a splinter group known as the Zealots believed that the defense of their religion called for resistance to and open rebellion against the conquerors. They would stop at nothing to put an end to Roman rule.

The other major party among the Jews was the Sadducees, represented chiefly by the rich and the priests. The Sadducees were not interested, as were the Pharisees, in the interpretation of the Torah; rather, they stressed ritual and a strict adherence to the letter of the law. Since the Torah said nothing about life after death, the Sadducees believed that people should be satisfied with life on earth alone. The Pharisees, on the contrary, gave some solace to the poor, who suffered hunger and oppression, by promising that for the righteous among them there would be a better life after death.

From both Sadducees and Pharisees, Herod demanded a loyalty oath, a promise that they would support his rule and not join the many conspirators who were plotting to assassinate him or overthrow him. As he grew older, Herod became insanely suspicious of opposition. He murdered his wife and had his mother-in-law executed for treason. He killed his brother-in-law, a legitimate heir, fearing that he might succeed him on the throne. He quarreled with his sons, exiling some of them to Rome, and when they came back, he put them in prison and executed them. (His cruelties led the Emperor Augustus to remark that he would rather be Herod's swine than his son—since pork was a forbidden item in the Jewish diet, pigs were not commonly butchered.)

When Herod discovered a plot to assassinate him, he executed all the citizens of Jerusalem who had been involved. The Jews were outraged, and one of his spies, the informant who had told about the plot, was caught by a mob and lynched in the streets. Herod tortured some women who had witnessed the scene, although they had not participated in it, until they told him who had been guilty, and then he executed the conspirators. He stationed spies everywhere in Jerusalem. Sometimes, he even disguised himself as a private citizen and went around the city talking to the common people, trying to get their candid opinions about him.

Most of the Sadducees, as members of a party that tried to get along well with whoever was in power, took the loyalty oath to Herod. But many of the Pharisees did not, even though they risked their lives by opposing the king. In many of the moves he made, Herod was rash, but he was not rash enough to force the Pharisee leaders to swear loyalty to him. He remembered the rebellions that had broken out against him before, and he was aware of the trouble that came to those who attempted to force the Jews to ignore their religious obligations. Herod knew that the vast majority of his subjects supported the Pharisees. For once he had to swallow his pride, and his suspicions, and leave his opponents unpunished.

Herod's introduction of Greco-Roman sports to the Holy Land horrified some Jews. In this Roman relief, spectators cheer two four-horse teams in a chariot race. The seven dolphins atop the arch at left mark the number of laps.

III

VOICES IN THE WILDERNESS

There was one religious group of Jews, as devout and as faithful to the ancient traditions as the Pharisees or the Sadducees, who posed no immediate threat to King Herod's rule. These were the Essenes, a group of men and women who had removed themselves from the rest of the nation and lived in separate communities. Many other Jews believed that the present state of affairs in Palestine would come to an end very soon and that a savior—the Messiah—would come to rescue the Jews from persecution and bring peace to the world. The Essenes, however, believed that it was important to dedicate themselves completely to preparing for his arrival. So they put aside all of their material concerns—the men abandoning their farms and shops, the women, their household cares—and waited for the new age. Herod found this situation quite satisfactory. The fewer of his subjects who wanted to interfere with his government the better he liked it.

The Essenes had first moved to Qumran, a hilltop on the west side of the Dead Sea, about a hundred years before Herod's time. A quarrel had arisen over which of the nation's priestly families had the right to provide the High Priest of the Temple at Jerusalem. One family, the Hasmonaeans, had the most power, for they had led the rebellion in 167 B.C. that re-established Jewish independence. They became high priests and later kings of the Jews as well. The supporters of the losing side—the Essenes—fled to the desert and set up a monastic community some miles north of Herod's fortress of Masada. These people refused

This animal-shaped pottery vessel was used in Palestine to store oil for household or ceremonial lamps.

Cave openings dot the sandstone cliffs at Qumran (opposite), near which the ancient Jewish sect the Essenes established their desert community.

43

THE DEAD SEA SCROLLS

Early in 1947 a Bedouin goatherd searching for a stray from his flock entered a cave in the steep cliffs of Jordan's Wadi Qumran and discovered large pottery jars containing tightly wrapped scrolls. He had accidentally stumbled upon the first cache of manuscripts that came to be called the Dead Sea Scrolls. The search for additional material since 1947 has uncovered at least eleven more caves containing hundreds of scrolls. After changing hands several times, the manuscripts of the first cave have found a permanent home in Israel. The Shrine of the Book (above right), in Jerusalem, is designed on the outside to simulate the top of the jar in which the first scrolls were found, and inside, the cave from which they came. The documents are displayed in a chamber beneath the dome. The Manual of Discipline (unrolled, far right) lists the rules of the Essene community at Qumran, which produced the scrolls. The tattered first sheet of the Thanksgiving Psalms (above) indicates the fragile condition of the scrolls. Restoring them and piecing together thousands of decayed fragments (right) has been the painstaking work of dedicated experts of all nationalities working at Jordan's Palestine Archaeological Museum as well as in Israel.

FREDERICK KIESLER AND ARMAND BARTOS, ARCHITECTS: PHOTOGRAPH BY EZRA STOLLER

45

to recognize the right of the victorious High Priest and his successors to offer sacrifices in the Temple. Their hatred of the Hasmonaeans was of course later shared by Herod, who had usurped the position of the old dynasty.

Eventually, the Essenes came to believe that they and their leaders had been given a special command by God to wait in the desert until the Messiah came. "In the wilderness, prepare the way of the Lord," the prophet Isaiah had written long before, "make straight in the desert a highway for our God." They also felt that their voluntary life in the wilderness was a re-enactment of the Israelites' wandering in the desert under Moses. Their forebears had waited to be shown the Promised Land of Canaan. Now the Essenes would strengthen and discipline themselves physically and morally during a similar waiting period.

By the time of Herod they had developed into a miniature replica of the entire Jewish nation. Ruled by their own priests, the Essenes performed their own religious ceremonies and conducted their own internal government. They even used their own calendar, one different from that used by the rest of the nation.

The Essenes considered themselves the advance guard of the troops who would battle against the forces of evil and usher in the reign of the Messiah. When the Messiah came, they believed, he would drive out the wicked Romans, who were growing rich on the labor of their subjects. Overthrowing the pagan gods, he would bring all the nations of the world together to worship in Jerusalem and to pray to the one true God of the Jews. In their belief in the eventual establishment of the kingdom of God on earth, the Essenes were no different from other Jews of the time.

Impoverished by Roman taxation and oppressed by Roman power, most of the Jewish nation looked forward in one way or another to the Messiah who would make them, instead of the Romans, the most powerful people in the world. Most of the Hebrews were desperately poor. In the countryside the farm workers often ate only vegetables, olives, and a little bread each day, for meat was a luxury that could be enjoyed only a few times a year. Often they were even too poor to buy firewood over which to cook their food. They went to a neighbor, less poor than they, who had water boiling over a fire and asked permission to dip in their vegetables just long enough to soften them for eating. Under these circumstances the Jews were eager for relief from the distress of their daily lives. They longed for the coming of the Messiah and the war they would wage against Rome.

Fifth-century mosaic panels exalting the fertility of nature decorate the pavement of the synagogue at Hammam Lif, Tunisia. A lion's head and a basket laden with bread are above. On the opposite page are an oryx (top) and a date palm.

To prepare themselves for that war, the Essenes, both men and women, lived like soldiers. They ate all their meals together, and they owned no individual property. The community controlled all the goods they used. Each member was issued his uniform, a simple white robe made of linen, which was worn by both men and women. The members were ordered into ranks and were under the strictest discipline. They were not allowed to interrupt while others were speaking or speak before those of higher rank did.

The Essenes' main settlement at Qumran was, by the time of Herod, a small city, completely self-supporting. It was so well protected from assault from any quarter that it had once been used as a fortress guarding against invasion of Judaea from across the Jordan River. Qumran's population lived in tents and in caves along the bluffs that line the barren shores of the Dead Sea, and the settlement spread for two miles north and south of the central group of buildings where the sect had its headquarters. Other Essenes lived in tents below the cliffs, right on the shore, and climbed up daily to pray and join in the communal meals.

Each day some of the members went out to tend the cattle or work in the fields, irrigating them with rain water that had been carefully collected in cisterns. Some worked at looms, weaving the white cloth for their robes, and others labored at kilns, making pottery for use in cooking and eating or for storage. Still others were assigned duties as scribes in the scriptorium, copying the Essenes' sacred writings on leather or papyrus. In fact, this work was kept going night and day. The extensive output of the scriptorium has only come to light since 1947, with the discovery and publication of the famous Dead Sea Scrolls.

Anyone who broke one of the rules of the sect was placed in a lower rank or, in serious cases, expelled from the community to fend for himself. If a member was exiled, he could easily starve to death, for he had taken a vow not to eat food that was grown by people outside the community. He might have to go out into the desert and eat whatever he could glean from the few plants that grew wild there. Anyone who broke the law prescribing rest on the Sabbath —even when he repented—was not re-admitted to full membership in the community for seven years.

Discipline among the Essenes was harsh, and their isolation was extraordinary. But there was a purpose behind it. The Essenes believed that the war to free Palestine from the Romans and usher in the reign of the Messiah would be fought on two fronts. One would be an outward battle be-

John the Baptist casts away his worldly attire to don a camel-hair cloak in this fifteenth-century Florentine painting by Domenico Veneziano, who depicted the Judaean wilderness as a bleak wasteland amid jagged mountains.

tween the Israelites and the invaders, fought with javelins and shields, bows and arrows, and siege engines and flame. The other battle would be an internal one within each individual, a struggle to follow the teachings of the Jewish law and to remain good. By keeping themselves separate from the rest of the world, they could be virtuous without distraction and carry on the second battle toward victory, even though the war with Rome had not yet begun.

The Essenes symbolized their difference from the rest of the world—their purity—with two rituals: their communal meals and their baptisms. At Qumran they ate together in a vast community hall about a hundred feet long. They remained completely silent until everyone was seated, and then one of the priests gave thanks for the food, as every pious Jew did before he ate, no matter how meager his fare was. The meal was considered to be an anticipation of the joyful gatherings that the faithful would have once the Messiah had come. Only those who had become pure enough in life were permitted to participate in these meals. In later years, when the Christian religion was established, the followers of Jesus gathered in a similar fashion to partake of bread and wine at sacred meals that re-enacted the Last Supper with his Disciples.

Before anyone could join the Essenes' common meals he had to be baptized, a rite symbolizing his purity. Among the Jews it had long been the custom to wash before prayers and meals. Indeed, it was a sin to eat food without washing one's hands, a custom that is widespread today but which in those days was rare even in civilized lands. The Jews also bathed to cleanse themselves when they had broken a religious law, and converts to Judaism also immersed themselves in water to wash away the defilement of idolatry. Priests too bathed before they sacrificed to God in the Temple. The Essenes took this custom and made it more important. To symbolize the new and holy life that he was embarking on, a new member dipped himself in flowing water, probably the Jordan River, which runs into the Dead Sea just a few miles from the settlement at Qumran.

The Essenes were not the only Jews to practice baptism. One holy man who also baptized people in the waters of the Jordan was John, called the Baptist, who was born around 4 B.C., the year of Herod's death. John, like many other holy men of the time, preferred to live alone in the wilderness, dedicated to meditation. He wore a camel-hair cloak and ate the hard, sweet, and nourishing fruit of the carob tree, which grew wild in the desert. Like the Essenes, John called on all the people to live holy lives, for he claimed that the Day of Judgment was at hand. Jews by the hundreds gathered from all over the land to hear him preach, and to be baptized in the Jordan River. They were asked to purify themselves before the coming of the Messiah, whom John conceived of as a heavenly judge, and to indicate their promise to live good lives from then on. John's followers walked right into the river; nowhere is it more than ten feet deep or more than one hundred feet wide, a little stream winding through the rocky desert countryside.

John was a stirring preacher. With his unkempt beard and his rough clothes, his face weathered and tanned by years of exposure to the desert sun, he must also have been a striking figure. And his uncompromising and stern command "Repent, for the kingdom of heaven is at hand" helped him gather a devoted following in the years around A.D. 25. To the Jews he was another of that line of fiery prophets who had long preached in Jerusalem and in the countryside of Palestine. As others before had done, he called on the people to follow the ethical teachings of the Torah as well as its ritual prescriptions.

The law of Moses contained two kinds of precepts. There were those that prescribed the ritual to be followed in the Temple and in daily life. Many were laws of diet: Jews were forbidden to eat the meat of the camel, the pig, and the rabbit. Others were laws about the Temple, indicating what animals and incense should be offered as sacrifices to God, when they should be offered, and by whom. Some were laws of property and laws that dealt with criminals. But there were also—and most important—the laws of conduct. The most famous of these are the Ten Commandments. There were many others, however, that required justice and concern, especially for the poor and helpless, and honesty in all dealings. It was not difficult for Jews, or anyone else for that matter, to keep from eating camel meat; it was more difficult for them, as for all men, to be kind and fair in everything they did. And throughout Jewish history, the prophets—men such as Nathan, Isaiah, and Micah—had come to remind the people of this, as the leaders of the Pharisees did too. With the end of the age

For much of its length the historic Jordan River is a shallow, meandering stream, as shown in the photograph opposite. The portrait above of John as a stern prophet is a detail from a fourteenth-century Byzantine fresco.

Herod's soldiers wrench infants from their mothers' arms in this vivid depiction of the Massacre of the Innocents from a Bulgarian manuscript prepared about 1356.

expected soon, the people were urged by John to reform—now it was more important than ever.

Thus, John was preaching justice, the Essenes were following their strict rule in preparation for the Day of Judgment, and the Pharisees in Jerusalem and elsewhere were teaching the people to stress the ethical part of the Mosaic law above all else. But the Romans and the princes of Herod's family were carrying on as usual.

Herod had died in 4 B.C. He had managed to hold power for more than thirty years, and he had served his Roman masters well by keeping peace—although an uneasy one—on the borders of Palestine and within the country itself. But he had not succeeded in convincing the Jews that Roman rule was best for them, and he had even less success in imposing Roman and Greek ways on the populace. Many religious Jews would not even enter the new cities, Sebaste and Caesarea, which Herod had built in Palestine. They were named for the Roman emperor and adorned with pagan temples. Many Jews refused to handle Roman coins because they had pictures of the emperor on them—an emperor who, to the scandal of the Jews, was worshiped as a god. In his last years, Herod had gone mad and had cruelly oppressed the people. Disregarding the Mosaic law against graven images, he had placed a golden eagle over the door to the Temple. His enemies, hearing Herod was on his deathbed, tore down the golden eagle as a gesture of defiance and hatred. But the old tyrant had enough breath in him to order the arrest and torture of the young men who committed the offense. There is even a story that when Herod was told, about this time, of the birth of the long-awaited Messiah, he ordered the murder of all male infants in Bethlehem; he wanted no rival. The tale of the Massacre of the Innocents seems to be in keeping with what is known about the demented old king's last years.

In an attempt to cure his painful final illness, Herod had himself rowed across the Dead Sea in order to bathe in the hot mineral springs on the far shore. When all else failed, he is said to have attempted suicide, but a relative prevented him from doing so. One of his last acts was to order the death of the imprisoned son he feared would succeed to his power. When he finally died and his kingdom was divided into three parts—one to each of his surviving sons—his subjects must have breathed enormous sighs of relief. A contemporary Jewish historian best expressed the feeling of the people for Herod: "He stole to the throne like a fox, he ruled like a tiger, and he died like a dog."

But none of his successors was any gentler than Herod himself had been. His son Herod Antipas, who ruled with the title of tetrarch in Galilee and the region east of the Jordan River, was especially tyrannical. When John the

A leering Herod Antipas pats the chin of his stepdaughter Salome in this medieval French stone carving.

53

Baptist began gathering throngs along the banks of the Jordan, Herod Antipas determined to get rid of the preacher. He feared that John's teaching would inspire a rebellion among his subjects, for the Jews found it hard to separate political and religious excitement and could not imagine that the Messiah would come without overthrowing the tyrants who were oppressing them. In fact, many were eager to hasten the coming of the Messianic Age by rebelling against the puppet rulers in anticipation of the great war. If the tyrants should be overthrown, even before the coming of the Messiah, they felt that their lives would be improved anyway. John had infuriated Herod Antipas by berating him for marrying his own sister-in-law, a woman who had been divorced from the ruler's half brother. Such a marriage was against the law of the Jews.

One day while John was preaching by the river, Herod Antipas sent his soldiers to arrest him and conduct him to the impregnable fortress of Machaerus on the shores of the Dead Sea, across from and south of the cliffs on which the Essene settlement stood. John was imprisoned for nearly a year while Herod Antipas decided what to do with him. He was inclined to leave John in prison where he could do no harm. Executing him was dangerous, for his followers might rebel. But Herodias, the prince's wife, thought differently. She was enraged by John's public proclamation that she was an adulteress. In the spring of A.D. 29 she

In this sixth-century Greek manuscript illumination a servant presents to Salome the head of John the Baptist as Herod and his guests look on from the banquet table. The tublike dungeon at right is conveniently open to expose two executioners with John's body. The figures of Moses (left) and King David (right) are in the margins.

found an opportunity to revenge herself on the preacher.

While she and Herod Antipas were at the fortress of Machaerus, which served as one of their royal palaces, the tetrarch's birthday occurred. The occasion was celebrated with a banquet in the great hall of the fortress, high above the dungeon where John lay imprisoned. As the banquet progressed, Herod Antipas got more and more drunk, and he finally called on his stepdaughter, Salome—Herodias' daughter by her first marriage—to dance before him and entertain the guests. The princess was reluctant to oblige him; she was young and, as an Oriental girl, sheltered. But Herod Antipas' requests became a demand, and finally he vowed that if Salome would dance he would give her anything she wanted, even if it was half his domain.

At this, Salome's mother took her aside and told her to do whatever Herod Antipas desired. As she danced she stripped off her veil, uncovering her face for all the company to see. In that time and at that place it was the same as appearing naked before the crowd. As soon as the dance was finished she bowed down before Herod Antipas and made the request her mother had coached her to make. It was the head of John the Baptist, brought before her on a platter, that she wanted. Herod Antipas was shocked; but the only thing he could do was grant the favor as he had promised. The order was sent to the dungeon beneath, and the preacher was beheaded by his prison guards. His head —still bleeding—was carried upstairs, where his triumphant enemy Herodias could see it before her, lying on the table in the midst of the food, while the guests continued to chatter and laugh and sing.

Herod Antipas had gotten rid of the troublesome preacher, and now, he hoped, there would no longer be any threat to the power of Rome. He decided that the people over whom he ruled were too concerned with religion anyway. If their religious leaders, who seemed to be causing all the trouble, were silenced, he reasoned, then the rebellion that threatened to break out might be avoided, and the population would remain peaceful. Religious belief had its place, in Herod Antipas' view, but it should be confined within the Temple walls or within the isolated communities of the Essenes, who bothered no one as long as they were left alone. But religious zealots such as John, who attracted large crowds throughout the countryside, were a different story. For the good of the public, and in the interest of Roman supremacy, these men would have to be suppressed, he decided, no matter how popular they were.

In this twelfth-century Coptic, or Egyptian Christian, illumination, John's baptism of Jesus is witnessed by hovering angels as God releases a dove, symbolizing the Holy Spirit. Fish, a symbol for Christ, dart up the Jordan.

IV

JESUS OF NAZARETH

A few weeks after John the Baptist had been beheaded in the dungeon at Machaerus, Herod Antipas and his family were startled by rumors that filtered into their palace. Reports reached them that John had not died, that some people who had known him well claimed to have seen him alive and proclaiming the same message he had once preached beside the Jordan River. Once again crowds were following him and listening with rapt attention to his message, for the story of John's miraculous rising from the dead was attracting thousands of people to see him.

In the city of Tiberias, which Herod Antipas had constructed on the shore of the Sea of Galilee and had named after the Roman Emperor Tiberius, the tetrarch listened to these astonishing tales with growing alarm. The accounts that came to him in his palace were confused ones. Some affirmed that it was true—that John had actually risen from the dead. Others reported that the preacher was not John at all but, just as amazing, the prophet Elijah, who had lived hundreds of years earlier. Others scoffed at these rumors and said that it was only Jesus of Nazareth, one of John's followers, who some persons now thought was the long-expected Messiah. Whoever the prophet was, he was preaching a message similar to that of John, promising the people that the kingdom of God was at hand. Many of them interpreted these sermons as a call for political change, and Herod Antipas decided that this man, like John, was dangerous.

The preacher had been gathering followers on the shore of the Sea of Galilee, near the town of Capernaum a few miles north of Tiberias, and in the hills beyond. But one day, while he was preaching on the shore of the lake, his followers warned him that Herod Antipas was inquiring about him. The preacher—it was, of course, Jesus and

Jesus' miracles are shown on this fifth-century Italian ivory panel. From top to bottom are the multiplying of the loaves and fishes; the restoring of the blind man's sight; and the curing of the palsied man, who takes up his pallet and walks.

not John or Elijah—was suspicious of the tetrarch's interest in his teaching. Getting into a boat, he asked to be rowed across the lake to find refuge outside the territory of Herod Antipas. Yet the crowds, determined to hear Jesus speak, followed him to Bethsaida. They spent most of the day walking in the hot sun for miles around the shore of the lake to reach the town and hear him finish his discourse.

In later years, when Jesus' followers formed a religion built around the belief that he was the Messiah, the story arose that Jesus had been born in Bethlehem, of a virgin mother, Mary, and was a descendant of King David, as the Messiah was supposed to be. This story was incorporated into two of the four Gospels, accounts of Jesus' life and teachings that were written between A.D. 70 and 100 and are attributed to Matthew, Mark, Luke, and John. These Gospels form the first four books of the Bible's New Testament. In these books, as elsewhere in both the Old and the New Testament, research done by Catholic, Protestant, and Jewish scholars has revealed that many stories, incidents, and speeches now in the Bible were added to the original tales in order to make their points stronger. The story of Jesus' birth in Bethlehem is probably one of these additions.

The Gospel according to Luke also reports that Jesus was John's kinsman. When John was preaching and baptizing converts by the Jordan River, Jesus, by then a man of thirty, arrived to hear him and was baptized as well. About the time of John's imprisonment in A.D. 28, Jesus returned to Galilee, but instead of going back to the central hills where his family lived, he went to the thickly populated western shore of the Sea of Galilee to preach to the people there.

Around him arose story after story of miracles performed—turning water into wine, driving demons from the possessed, making the blind see, raising the dead. The Gospel according to Luke recounts that the day the crowd followed him around the shore of the Sea of Galilee to Bethsaida, Jesus performed one of his most famous miracles. As evening drew on, his Disciples warned him that such a multitude would need food and lodging. "You give them something to eat," Jesus commanded. "We have no more than five loaves and two fish . . ." they protested. It was ridiculous to think of feeding the five thousand who were now gathered with so little. But Jesus told them to bid the crowd be seated, in groups of fifty each. Then, after blessing the meager supply of loaves and fishes, he miraculously multiplied them and gave them to the Disciples to be distributed among the people. The leftovers, according to Luke, filled twelve baskets.

Similar stories of miracles had been told about prophets among the Jews in the past. Elsewhere, in other times, great religious leaders, Mohammed and Buddha most notably, were also said to have performed miracles. In these same years and later, certain Jewish teachers in addition to Jesus had the reputation of being able to heal the sick and work other wonders. But, as the number of stories of Jesus' mighty works multiplied and reached village after village, the crowds who followed him increased.

Most of his followers were unlearned peasants, the *am ha-aretz*, or "people of the land"; but they were devout. They had listened raptly to John and to the other wandering preachers who announced the imminent end of the age. In lakeside villages, on the Sabbath or in the evening, while the scholars and those men who could read gathered in one corner of the synagogue to discuss the fine points of the Jewish law, the poorer and less educated men huddled outside talking excitedly about the rumors that swept through the countryside. The outbreak of rebellion in the hills of Galilee; the assassination of a Roman official; the miraculous healing of a sick man—all these signs, they speculated, seemed to point toward the coming of the Messiah.

One day Jesus encountered two fishermen, Simon, called Peter, and his brother Andrew, whom he had first met among the followers of John the Baptist. They were at work in their boats close to the shore, casting nets into the water for fish when Jesus asked them to join him as Disciples. "Follow me," he said, "and I will make you fishers of men." Abandoning their work, they eagerly agreed to go.

The Pharisees scorned people like Jesus' Disciples Peter and Andrew, who had neither the knowledge nor the inclination to observe all of the hundreds of detailed prescriptions of the Jewish law. But to Jesus, the law was less important. Like the prophets who had preceded him, Jesus did preach the observance of the law, and like them he stressed its inner content rather than just its outer form. Yet there were some ways in which his teaching differed from Jewish law and called for significant changes.

The Pharisees and the Sadducees believed that following the ethical and ritual commandments of the Jewish law was in itself enough to make men good. Jesus also stressed the importance of the Torah, but he felt that regardless of the law, man could know what was right to do. "Think not that I have come to abolish the law and the prophets," he

A second ivory panel depicts three other miracles of Jesus', including the raising of a shrouded Lazarus from the dead (top); the changing of water into wine at the wedding feast in Cana (center); and the healing of a spotted leper (bottom).

THE NATIVITY

The birth of Jesus, as recounted in the New Testament Gospels, has been a source of inspiration to artists through the centuries. In Luke's version, the tale begins with the appearance of the angel Gabriel to Mary, a virgin of Nazareth betrothed to Joseph. "Do not be afraid, Mary, for you have found favor with God," the angel says in announcing that she is to be the mother of Jesus. The incident is depicted at left in an eleventh-century French drawing. Opposite, the early fourteenth-century Italian painter Giotto recreates the traditional Nativity scene, with Mary and the infant Jesus lying in a Bethlehem manger as Joseph rests in the foreground and angels rejoice above. Matthew's story ends with the presentation of gifts to Jesus by three wise men of the East. In the stained-glass window from France's Chartres Cathedral below, an angel warns the Magi not to tell Herod, who wishes to harm Jesus, of their visit.

proclaimed in the Sermon on the Mount, "I have come not to abolish them but to fulfill them." The difference between the Jewish teachers and Jesus—and the difference between Judaism and Christianity over the centuries—was never in what they wanted of the people. The best men in both religions strove for obedience to what they believed to be the will of God. They differed rather in their judgment of how to achieve this goal.

Jesus' teaching also departed from standard Jewish practice about the Sabbath. One Saturday he and his Disciples were walking through a grainfield, and the Disciples stopped to pick some ears of grain. When he was reproached because his Disciples were breaking the law that forbade work such as harvesting on the Sabbath, Jesus answered: "The sabbath was made for man, not man for the sabbath. . ." He also disagreed with Jewish laws permitting divorce, claiming that the only just cause for divorce was adultery. Furthermore, he declared that no person should ever take a sacred oath. A man's word alone should be his bond.

Jesus taught that all men should base their actions on love. "Love your enemies, do good to those who hate you, bless those who curse you, pray for those who abuse you," he said to his followers. "To him who strikes you on the cheek, offer the other also; and from him who takes away your cloak do not withhold your coat as well . . . as you wish that men would do to you, do so to them. If you love those who love you, what credit is that to you? For even sinners love those who love them. And if you do good to those who do good to you, what credit is that to you? For even sinners do the same. And if you lend to those from whom you hope to receive, what credit is that to you? Even sinners lend to sinners, to receive as much again. But love your enemies, and do good, and lend, expecting nothing in return; and your reward will be great . . ."

Yet many of Jesus' followers found it difficult to accept his message. What they wanted most was a political Messiah, a divinely sent king who would drive the Romans out of the country. The crowds who came to hear him, and even the Disciples who followed him closely, pleaded for a sign from Jesus indicating that he was sent by God to end Roman power and usher in the rule of God. Jesus was not the only man to inspire such hopes in the populace. Some twenty years after his death, a man named Theudas, who claimed to be the Messiah, gathered a great many people around him. He led them down to the Jordan River and promised to perform a miracle: he would cause the muddy

In this illustration from a German Gospel book, Jesus sleeps through a storm on the Sea of Galilee. A worried Apostle attempts to rouse Jesus so he can quell the tempest.

The sixth-century mosaic at left from Ravenna, Italy, depicts Jesus summoning Simon Peter and Andrew from their nets. Fishermen today still anchor their boats on the shores of the Sea of Galilee (below). Usually calm, the sea is also known for sudden, violent storms.

63

Of that excellent sermon of our lorde Ihū in þe hil Capitulit. xviii:

Whan our Lord Ihū had chose and gadered his disciples as is ī seide willyng to teche hem and enfoorme hem yn þe pfection of þe new law: he lad he led hem vp in to an hill þat is clepid Thabr a boute two myle fro nazareth aftr þe coñoñ opynyoñ and þ he made to hem a long sermoñ and ful of swetnes as Señte Austyne saith here

begynnyng of his boke þat he made of þat sermoñ it conteynyth al the pfection of cristen lyvyng for þat sermoñ he taucte hem firste which men bene blessid of god and worthy to haue his blisse Also he taucte hem þe trew maner of preyer of fastynge and of almes dede and other vtues longyng to þe pfite lif of man as the texte of þat gospol openlio tellyth And dyvers doctours and clerkis expownen it sufficientlio þe which presse we passe on her for as mych as it is writen bope ī latyñe and in englissh in mony oþer waters of the river to divide, leaving dry land so that the people could walk over to the other side. The Romans sent out a troop of cavalry that attacked the crowd of hopeful people, killing or wounding many of them. Theudas was seized and executed and his head displayed in Jerusalem as a warning to anyone who might attempt to mislead the people by rebelling against Rome.

Jesus' followers came to believe that he really was the Messiah. His ability to work miracles, they thought, could be used to drive out the Romans and bring an end to the sufferings of the Jews. In some ways, Jesus encouraged this feeling by refusing to deny that he was indeed the Messiah. But to proclaim himself openly as the Messiah would take the heart out of his teachings. People were supposed to heed his message and act in accordance with it not because he was the Messiah but simply because it was the righteous and just thing to do.

Some of his followers offered Jesus the title of king and urged him to make war on Rome. They were eager for him to do so not only for religious reasons but because some among them hoped to share in his political power. But Jesus refused to lead them in rebellion, and many of his disappointed followers began to desert him.

To hold together the disenchanted among his Disciples, Jesus at last told them that he was the Messiah but charged them to reveal it to no one. Nevertheless, rumors that Jesus was, or claimed to be, the Messiah continued to spread. Herod Antipas and the Romans, afraid that an insurrection might break out, grew extremely uneasy. The tetrarch was concerned about Jesus' potential influence, and he decided to put him to death. Although the Pharisees opposed some of Jesus' teachings, they came to warn him of the danger. Jesus finally decided to leave Galilee and go to Jerusalem, most likely in the year 29.

Although some biblical accounts compress the story of Jesus' stay in Jerusalem to one brief week, it probably lasted a few months. Each day he went to the Temple to preach to the people who congregated in its courtyard. There, as in Galilee, he attracted many followers; there too he debated with the Pharisees and the Sadducees.

His independent preaching was already disturbing reli-

Flanked by Old Testament figures Moses and Elijah, Jesus is transfigured in a holy light on Mount Tabor. On the slopes below, in this 1220 Syrian Gospel illustration, three Apostles witness the vision.

The fifteenth-century English illuminated manuscript opposite shows Jesus delivering the Sermon on the Mount to an enrapt audience. During this discourse, Jesus recited the famous lesson that is known as the Beatitudes.

A low morning haze begins to lift from a hillside village on the outskirts of Jeru-

salem. *The countryside surrounding the city is little changed from Jesus' time.*

gious leaders of the nation, who felt that interpreters of the law should undergo a long and rigorous course of study before they were qualified to teach. Other statements added to their resentment. "Again I tell you, it is easier for a camel to go through the eye of a needle than for a rich man to enter the kingdom of God." This pronouncement was a barbed criticism of the wealthy Sadducees.

At the Temple, Jews who came from abroad had to exchange their foreign coins—which had pictures of gods or the emperor on them—for coins issued by the city of Tyre in Phoenicia. These coins were the only legal currency that could be used to purchase the birds, oxen, and sheep offered as sacrifices. Jesus protested strongly against this commerical traffic in the house of God, antagonizing the Sadducees, who profited from such transactions and who considered them to be necessary for efficient operation of the Temple. In the Gospel according to John, it becomes a dramatic story. There it is claimed that Jesus took a whip and scourged the moneychangers and overthrew the tables on which they conducted their business, spilling their coins on the Temple pavement.

Jesus thought it more important to teach the ignorant and the sinful than those who were already learned and good. This scandalized the Pharisees, who prided themselves on avoiding all contact with sinners or unlearned people and who claimed that it was best to spend time only with those who were as good or better than oneself. But Jesus scoffed at those among the Pharisees who objected to his behavior. He called them hypocrites and accused them of being more interested in minor points of the law than they were in the morality that underlay the law. The Pharisees, of course, did not agree with this view of themselves.

An illustration from the Rossano Gospels, a rare sixth-century service book in Greek, shows Jesus driving vendors from the Temple. He chastises two at left as others with their wares flee his wrath.

According to the Gospels, Jesus entered Jerusalem on Palm Sunday surrounded by crowds shouting hosannas. In the twelfth-century Greek illumination at left, two children frolic along his path while several elders await him at the city gates.

Like the Sadducees, they came to think of Jesus as a dangerous radical who was determined to overthrow the law and substitute his own teaching for it. To them the law was immeasurably precious, for it embodied what they considered to be the only true religion, the only religion revealed to man by God. Slowly it became evident that just as Jesus had been in danger from Herod Antipas in Galilee, he was now in danger from the Jewish religious authorities in Jerusalem. Once more he had to retire to safety, this time to Peraea, on the other side of the Jordan.

But, at the time of Passover, in the spring of the year 30, when Jewish pilgrims came from everywhere to visit the Temple, Jesus returned to the Holy City. He probably hoped to preach to the crowds and inspire the entire Jewish people with his teachings. But by then it was too late, for his fate was already sealed. Alerted to his return, his enemies, who had long resented Jesus' popularity, had gone to the Roman governor, Pontius Pilate. They convinced him that Jesus, who considered himself the Messiah, was a dangerous figure and could easily lead an insurrection among the Jews. Pilate listened carefully to their warning. Palestine was seething with disaffection, and he himself

Jesus washes the feet of his Disciples in the illustration at left from the Rossano Gospels. According to John's Gospel, Jesus' act of humility occurred at his last meal with his Disciples. At right Giotto's fresco of the Last Supper shows all the Disciples with halos except Judas (at far left).

was extremely unpopular. Rebellion was in the air, and it could easily break out at a time such as Passover. Thousands of Jews were gathered in Jerusalem, where everything in the city reminded them of the glory of their own tradition and of the hated power of Rome.

Jesus was aware of his danger. He and his Disciples celebrated the Seder, the traditional Passover feast of the Jews, together. In this—their last supper—as they ate unleavened bread and drank wine, Jesus warned them of the mortal peril he faced. After the meal he went outside the city walls to Gethsemane, a garden in the valley below the slopes of the Mount of Olives. While he was praying there—in the company of a few of his Disciples—a group of men armed with swords and clubs came to arrest him.

"Have you come out as against a robber, with swords and clubs to capture me?" Jesus asked them. "Day after day I was with you in the temple teaching, and you did not seize me."

But the answer to his question was an obvious one. If he had been arrested during the day, in public, a riot might have broken out, a riot that might have led to a full-scale rebellion. As it was, his Disciples attempted to fight back in the garden of Gethsemane. According to John's Gospel, Peter even cut off the ear of the High Priest's slave, who was among those taking Jesus into custody. But the few followers who were with him in the garden were no match for the men, and Jesus was taken away.

From the garden of Gethsemane, the crowd led Jesus back within the city walls and into the house of the High Priest, a man named Joseph, the son of Caiaphas. Like many of the other Sadducees, Joseph ben Caiaphas was eager to conciliate Pontius Pilate and the Romans, and

70

he was also anxious to stamp out any signs of rebellion.

The examination by the High Priest had to take place hurriedly. If Jesus was to be turned over to the Romans for execution as a potential rebel, it had to be done immediately. It was a Thursday night, and Passover was about to begin. If a criminal was not punished by sundown Friday, a week would have to go by before his trial and execution could be held, for the Passover festival was too sacred to allow the taking of life. And if Jesus was allowed to remain in prison for a week, the people might demand his release, or rebel anyway.

The Sanhedrin was called into session—the same group that had tried Herod many years before. During Herod's trial, it had been controlled by the Pharisees, who were interested in preserving the life of every man, criminal or not. But under Herod and his successors, it had become a stronghold of the Sadducees, who were much more harsh than other Jews in applying the law.

The examination of Jesus went quickly. At that time the Sanhedrin had no right to pass a sentence of death. It could only decide whether a criminal was guilty and deserved imprisonment or flogging or whether the case was serious enough to call for the death penalty. If the latter was so, then the Sanhedrin passed the criminal on to Roman authorities for trial and judgment.

According to the account in the Gospels, the examination took place at night on the same evening that Jesus was arrested. In their long robes, the men of the Sanhedrin filed into the large chamber where their meetings were held, a room lit only by flickering lamps. Witnesses were summoned against Jesus, and they claimed that they had heard him say he would destroy the Temple. Jesus refused to confirm or deny the charge, which enraged the Sanhedrin against him, for many of them held high positions in the Temple. But this accusation alone was certainly not enough to merit a death sentence. Other Jews, religious fanatics who made similar statements, were merely whipped through the streets of Jerusalem and let go free. But then the High Priest asked Jesus the crucial question: Was he the Messiah? If Jesus answered yes, it meant to these Sadducees only one thing—that he was planning to lead a rebellion against Rome. Here Jesus broke his silence for the first time during the examination and answered the High Priest indirectly: "You have said so." This was not an incriminating answer. It could mean yes, or it could merely be a restatement of the question. Jesus refused to

Seen through the tombstones of an Arab cemetery in this photograph of modern Jerusalem is the Franciscan Church of All Nations in the garden of Gethsemane; beyond it, on the slopes of the Mount of Olives, is an onion-domed Russian Orthodox church.

deny that he was indeed the Messiah, but he chose a safe
way of saying something that could be very dangerous if it
were spoken directly. Yet a moment later he did speak
more openly. He announced to the High Priest that soon he
would see him—Jesus—sitting in glory at the right hand of
God. When the High Priest heard Jesus claim that he, a
mere man, would sit next to God, he solemnly made a tear
in his robe of office, as was the custom whenever anyone
was heard to utter a blasphemy. The High Priest interpreted Jesus' earlier answer as a claim to be the Messiah
and thus a rebel against Rome. He therefore had to be
handed over to the Roman authorities for judgment. When
the members of the Sanhedrin who were in attendance had

An early fourteenth-century painting by Duccio records the events of Jesus' arrest in Gethsemane. Peter (left) lops off

a man's ear as Judas plants his kiss of betrayal—the signal for arrest. The remaining Disciples (right) flee in terror.

At the top of this Rossano Gospel page Jesus and his accusers appear before Pilate. Below, after the High Priest scorns Judas' attempt to return the silver pieces taken for betraying Jesus, the Disciple hangs himself (right).

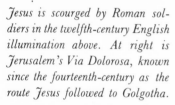

Jesus is scourged by Roman sol-diers in the twelfth-century English illumination above. At right is Jerusalem's Via Dolorosa, known since the fourteenth-century as the route Jesus followed to Golgotha.

agreed with the High Priest, Jesus was led out of the room, bound, and put into prison for the remainder of the night. Early the next morning, he would appear before Pilate.

As dawn broke, he was conducted through the narrow, deserted streets of Jerusalem to the palace, on the eastern side of the city, where Pilate was staying. The governor had come up to the city to witness the celebration of the Pass-over festival and to be on hand in case any trouble broke out among the pilgrims who were crowding into the town. The Bible story is filled with many details of Jesus' trial before Pilate. It recounts how Pilate tried hard to set Jesus free, that he was sympathetic to him and only condemned him to crucifixion because the Jews insisted on getting rid of Jesus. Actually very little is known of what went on at the Jewish examination and the Roman trial. The accounts of them in the Gospels were written years later, at a time when the followers of Jesus were trying to win friends in the Roman world and wanted to disclaim any connection with Rome's enemies, the rebellious Jews. The story is written

77

Andrea Mantegna, a fifteenth-century Italian artist, incorporated many written and oral traditions about the Crucifixion in the panoramic painting at right. Jesus awaits his death on the cross at Golgotha, the place of a skull—so called, according to one theory, because of the hill's rounded shape. Roman guards (right) toss dice for Jesus' cloak while a nearly prostrate Mary (left) is supported by women followers of her son. At the extreme left, the Disciple John suffers his master's agony. In the background a road winds to a Jerusalem resembling an Italian hill city.

in such a way as to condemn the Jews and favor the Romans. But from what is known of Pontius Pilate from writings outside the Bible, it seems evident that he was a man to whom the life of one suspected rebel would be unimportant; he was a man who was strongly determined to demonstrate the power of Rome to the Jews, and it is unlikely that he would ever have thought of letting Jesus go free. When Jesus was brought before him, Pilate probably condemned him quickly and ordered his execution on the same day.

The sentence was crucifixion, a barbarously cruel punishment that the Romans reserved for slaves and those whom they considered to be the lowest criminals—rebels and traitors. The Romans had few qualms about human suffering. Not only did they hang condemned criminals on the cross, but before crucifying their prisoners, the Romans scourged them with thongs or with whips to which pieces of lead had been attached.

As soon as Pilate had pronounced judgment, Jesus was taken outside and scourged by the Roman soldiers. After the scourging his flesh was raw and bleeding; but according to Roman custom, like all other condemned criminals, he had to carry the crossbeam on which he would die through the streets of the city to the place of execution. In Jerusalem, this was a hill called Golgotha, just outside the walls. No execution was permitted within the walls of the Holy City, close to the Temple.

For part of the way Jesus was able to carry the crossbeam. After a while, however, he began to stumble under its great weight, and a passer-by named Simon, a North African Jew from the city of Cyrene who was visiting Jerusalem as a pilgrim, was hailed by the Roman troops and ordered to carry the beam the rest of the way.

The Romans usually carried a sign before each condemned criminal announcing the crime of which he was guilty. Jesus' sign read "The King of the Jews," showing that he was accused of planning a rebellion against Rome. This sign, in Latin, Greek, and Aramaic, the common language of the Palestinian Jews, was probably fixed to the beam. To mock Jesus, the Roman soldiers had also made a crown of thorns and flowers and put it on his head, as if it were the crown of a king. As the procession moved along through the streets, a group of Jerusalem women who aided condemned criminals offered him a drink of vinegar mixed with myrrh. The drink was supposed to serve as a partial anesthetic to dull his senses and diminish his pain as he hung on the cross; but Jesus refused to take the potion.

While followers of Jesus prepare his body for the tomb an incense-bearing angel watches over them in this medieval French miniature.

When the small procession came to Golgotha, the cross-beam was fixed to an upright pole already standing. Jesus was then raised upon the cross, tied there with rope, and probably nailed to it as well. For six hours he hung there in the hot sun, with flies buzzing about his raw wounds and the women among his followers grieving a short distance away. His male Disciples, except possibly John, did not dare come to Golgotha to witness the execution, for they too might have been seized by the Romans and punished as rebels. Jesus' cross was flanked by two others, on each of which hung a man also accused of rebellion.

As the day progressed, Jesus grew weaker and weaker, and for a moment despair seized him. "My God, my God, why hast thou forsaken me?" he called out. But as he came closer to death, despair left him, and he asked God to pardon those who had condemned him to death. "Father, forgive them for they know not what they do." Finally, with a loud cry, he died, and the women who were waiting beneath the cross began to wail the ancient chants of mourning with which Jews commemorate their dead.

It is reported in the New Testament that the man who claimed the body of Jesus, Joseph of Arimathea, was a member of the Sanhedrin. It was in Joseph's empty tomb that Jesus' body was placed. The tombs of the Sanhedrin (left) in Jerusalem are very likely similar to the burial place of Jesus.

AFTER THE CRUCIFIXION

At dawn on the Sunday following the death of Jesus, Mary Magdalene—accompanied by one or two other women disciples—went out to the sepulcher, where he had been hastily laid to rest, in order to anoint his body properly. The four Gospels differ in minor detail about what the women saw at the tomb, but all state that Jesus was gone, that he had risen from the dead. The Resurrection of Jesus is a central doctrine of Christianity; to believers it proves that he was indeed the Messiah sent from God. In the tempera altarpiece opposite, by the early Renaissance painter Duccio, an angel sitting on the empty tomb announces the miracle to the three women. One among the elated Disciples refused to believe the tale until Jesus, appearing to the assembled Apostles, allowed him to touch his wounds. The story of doubting Thomas is depicted in the Arab manuscript illustration above at left. Forty days after the Resurrection, Luke's book The Acts of the Apostles relates, Jesus was taken up to heaven. A fifth-century Roman Christian artist combined the Resurrection and Ascension in a single ivory panel, above right. At the bottom of the panel, the angel at the tomb addresses the three women; at the top, an ascending Jesus takes the outstretched hand of God while one Apostle cowers in fright and another stares in awe.

Outside the wall of the city of Damascus, Jesus appears to Paul. In this 1410 French illumination, Paul's horse also seems to be affected by the vision.

FIRST CHRISTIAN

Many Jews were wholly unconcerned with the religious revival that men like Jesus and John the Baptist were preaching, and many cared little about the prospect of fighting to liberate their country from Rome. These people wanted only to be left alone. They believed that Judaism could survive, even under Roman rule, as long as the Jews continued to study and observe the law.

In the eyes of most Jews, studying the Torah was the most worthwhile occupation a man could follow. Jerusalem was the great center of religious studies, and to the city each year came hundreds of young men from Palestine and abroad, eager to steep themselves in the ancient traditions and to learn the biblical laws by heart. A few years after Jesus' crucifixion, one such scholar, a young man named Saul, set out for Jerusalem from his home in Tarsus, a prosperous riverside city on the southeastern coast of Asia Minor, in what is now Turkey. As a Jew living among pagans, Saul had learned the names and characteristics of the pagan gods and had seen the sacrifices that were performed in their honor. But, like most of the Jews of the Diaspora who lived outside of their ancient homeland, he maintained a fervent devotion to his own religion.

Sometime around A.D. 33, he arrived in the Holy City to study with the famous Pharisee leader Rabbi Gamaliel. He probably went first to a synagogue where other men from Tarsus and the towns nearby gathered to worship. Then, as soon as he had found a place to stay, he set out to find work, for it was a tradition among the Pharisees that all scholars and teachers earn their living through labor. Some were shoemakers and others were tailors; some did heavier work—chopping wood or carrying burdens in the market place. Saul was a weaver and a tentmaker—or perhaps a leatherworker—by trade. To make a living he had to find a craftsman who needed an extra worker, or perhaps he merely set up a wooden loom he had brought from home

and worked alone. Only then could he present himself to Rabbi Gamaliel.

Saul was one of several pupils who sat at the rabbi's feet, listening to complex discussions about the application of the law. Short and dark-haired, with glowing eyes and an intense manner, Saul was an opinionated student. He soon found that he disagreed with Gamaliel, who believed that the strict interpretation of the law was unnecessary. Like most Pharisees, Gamaliel encouraged stretching the law a bit when the needs of men required it, for the Torah, they believed, was made for man, not man for the Torah. Saul, on the other hand, remained convinced that anyone who did not obey the law completely, down to the last letter, was condemned.

A short while before Saul had come to Jerusalem, Jesus' Disciple Peter had been brought before Gamaliel and the other elders of the Sanhedrin for trial. Peter, like Jesus' other followers, was teaching that Jesus was the Messiah; that he had risen from the dead and ascended to heaven; and that he would soon return to earth to establish the kingdom of God. Many members of the Sanhedrin were scandalized at this. They considered it blasphemous, and they wanted to exile or punish Peter and the other Nazarenes, as the followers of Jesus were then known. But Gamaliel rose before the court and defended them. "Have nothing to do with these men, let them be," he argued. "If this is man's design or man's understanding, it will be overthrown; if it is God's, you will have no power to overthrow it."

Saul, however, was not as tolerant as his teacher. When an outraged Jerusalem mob seized the Nazarene Stephen, who was harshly berating the crowd for disregarding Jesus, and stoned him to death, Saul stood by, encouraging the murder. It was the first incident in a general persecution, and many of Jesus' followers fled from Jerusalem to Damascus for refuge. Saul, " . . . breathing threats and murder against the disciples . . ." as recorded in the Acts of the Apostles, went to the High Priest and asked for letters to the synagogues of Damascus. He was determined to stamp out the sect. If he found any Nazarenes trying to make converts among the Jews, he would ask the Damascus author-

Destroyed, rebuilt, and destroyed again over the centuries, Jerusalem today reflects the architectural styles of many eras and many cultures. The arch over the Old City street opposite shows the influence of Arab rulers.

Stephen, accused of blasphemy by the Jews of Jerusalem, is stoned to death outside the city walls in the ninth-century Byzantine manuscript illustration at left. Paul (at right, with a halo) is a spectator. The events surrounding Paul's conversion are seen in the ninth-century Bible illumination opposite. At top, Paul is struck, then felled, by the vision and arises blind. At center, Ananias receives God's command to heal Paul, and he restores the Apostle's sight (right). In the bottom panel, Paul preaches to a group of likely converts.

ities to let him bring the troublemakers back to Jerusalem as prisoners.

The High Priest gave Saul the authority to go to Damascus to suppress the new cult. With two companions, he set out for the land beyond the Sea of Galilee, crossing the high and arid plain that led to the great Syrian city. As he was proceeding upon the road, an astonishing thing occurred. The New Testament book of Acts tells the story: "... suddenly a light from heaven flashed about him. And he fell to the ground and heard a voice saying to him, 'Saul, Saul, why do you persecute me?' And he said, 'Who are you, Lord?' And he said, 'I am Jesus, whom you are persecuting . . .' The men who were traveling with him stood speechless, hearing the voice but seeing no one. Saul arose from the ground; and when his eyes were opened, he could see nothing; so they led him by the hand and brought him into Damascus."

This vision, which Saul believed to be supernatural, a miracle sent by God, marked a major step in the development of Christianity. Saul had found his mission; there-

after, he was an ardent believer in Jesus. All the energy and emotion he had previously devoted to persecuting the Nazarenes was now to be dedicated to advancing their cause.

When he regained his sight in Damascus, Saul made contact with the very people he had come to persecute. He was baptized and spent most of the next three years in the city, practicing his trade and preaching. To symbolize the great change in his life, it is said, the convert even changed his name. No longer was he Saul—with the same name as an ancient king of Israel—but rather Paul, a far more humble name, for it comes from a Latin word meaning "little." Actually, it is more likely that Paul had three names: Shaul, or Saul, in Hebrew and Aramaic; Paulos in Greek; Paulus in Latin. It might therefore have been convenient for him to use his name in the language of the country he was living in. Later when he left Judaea to travel widely throughout the Roman Empire, he came to use the nearly identical Greek or Roman names in preference to the Hebrew Saul.

Despite his new association with the humble followers of Jesus, humility was a difficult thing for Paul to practice. He was a forceful man, and his uncompromising nature made him many enemies. After a time, he found that Damascus was no longer a safe place for the practice of the new faith. Word came that the Jews wanted him arrested, and he escaped from the city by being lowered over the wall in a basket.

He made his way back to Jerusalem—very likely in the year A.D. 36—but he was only able to remain there for a brief time. The Jerusalem Nazarenes viewed him with suspicion. They remembered him as an enemy; now he came to them as an ally, and they were not sure they could trust him. Moreover, because he had not been one of the original followers of Jesus, there was no place for him there as a leader among the Nazarenes. Soon he left the city and returned to his native Tarsus. He was to remain away from Jerusalem for a decade, years in which he slowly and painfully evolved into a different person, a man who was far more gentle than the youth Saul had been. Paul was still capable of criticizing harshly those he considered enemies, but he was now more concerned with gaining friends than in arguing with opponents. His conversion had been sudden and swift; like all great changes, it took years of work before it finally became complete.

Toward the end of this decade, Paul visited Antioch, in Syria, one of the largest and most famous cities of the an-

For a 1470 manuscript, a traveler to the Middle East drew Damascus as a multistoried, fortified city.

cient world. There, in a fertile river valley, surrounded by miles of orchards and vineyards, a mixed population of Greeks and Syrians, Romans and Jews, carried on an extensive trade with many lands of the Mediterranean area.

In this cosmopolitan city, Paul joined forces with the followers of Jesus who had already established a congregation in the town. There, unlike Jerusalem, the gentile believers were as important in the government of the church as were the Jews. Paul soon gained a position of predominance in the community as hundreds of people—gentiles and Jews—came to hear him preach in Greek, the common language of the city, and of the entire eastern half of the Roman Empire. His message was a strong one. He proclaimed that Jesus was the Messiah, the Son of God, who

Paul seems to be riding a swing in this ninth-century Italian fresco. In reality, the Apostle is escaping from Damascus in a basket.

had come to earth to redeem mankind from sin and who would return to establish the kingdom of God. If a man believed this, his sins would be forgiven and his salvation assured. If he denied it, then his opportunity for redemption was lost.

It was here in Antioch that Jesus' followers came to be called Christians for the first time. The name comes from the Greek word *Christos*, which means "anointed" or "messiah." Yet, although the believers at Antioch were the first to be called Christians, Paul himself actually deserves the title of the first Christian. For it was he who really made the break between the followers of Jesus and the Jews who remained faithful to their religion. The original Disciples of Jesus, and Jesus himself, considered themselves to be Jews, and they expected all of their followers to adhere to the Jewish law. But the laws of Judaism were difficult to observe. Soon there arose a class of gentiles who were sympathetic to the new faith but who were unwilling to undertake all of its obligations under the Judaic code.

Many of the Jewish followers of Jesus were unsure of how they should deal with these gentile converts. Should gentiles also be required to be circumcised and to observe the Jewish dietary laws? And if they were not required to observe these dietary laws, should gentiles be permitted to join Jews in the ceremonial meals that in time came to symbolize Jesus' Last Supper? James, who was the leader of the Jerusalem church, and the most respected of all the early Nazarenes, was determined to preserve the link with Judaism. He did not insist on circumcision, but he was adamant in upholding the dietary laws and in refusing to take part in common meals with gentiles. Paul, on the other hand, believed that Judaism had been superseded by the coming of Jesus. Neither circumcision nor dietary laws were necessary in the new religion, Paul taught.

Paul discussed these problems with James and Peter in A.D. 46 when he visited Jerusalem, heading a delegation from Antioch that was bringing food to the Nazarenes in the Holy City, then gripped by famine. Peter, whom Jesus himself had chosen as an Apostle, wavered in his adherence to the Jewish law. Paul quarreled bitterly with Peter, who had eaten meals with gentile converts at first but then changed his mind and refused to eat with anyone who did not observe the Jewish law. Paul saw that this was dangerous; it would quickly lead to the formation of two sects— Jewish Christians and gentile Christians. There was the added danger that Christianity would be reduced to a mere

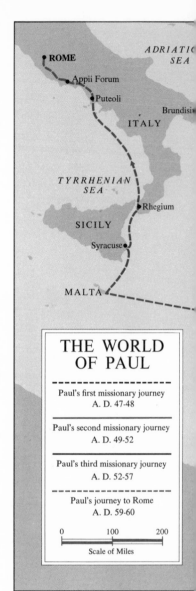

THE WORLD OF PAUL

Paul's first missionary journey
A. D. 47-48

Paul's second missionary journey
A. D. 49-52

Paul's third missionary journey
A. D. 52-57

Paul's journey to Rome
A. D. 59-60

0   100   200
Scale of Miles

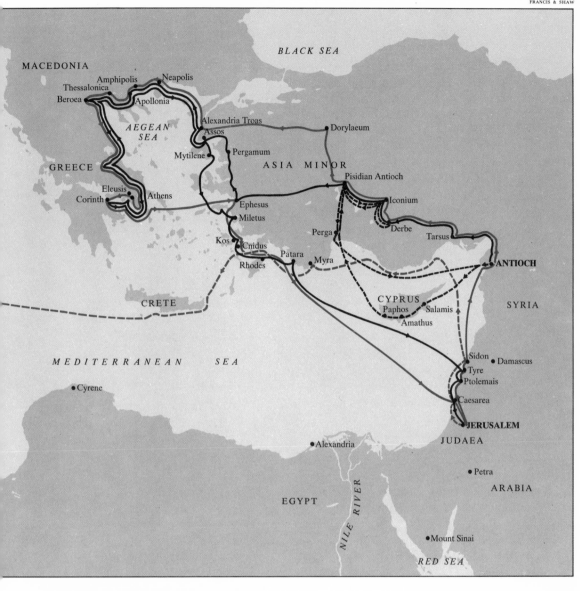

BLACK SEA

MACEDONIA

Amphipolis   Neapolis
Thessalonica
Beroea   Apollonia

AEGEAN
SEA

Alexandria Troas
Assos

Mytilene   Pergamum

GREECE

ASIA MINOR

Pisidian Antioch

Iconium

Eleusis   Athens   Ephesus
Corinth   Miletus

Perga   Derbe

Tarsus

Kos   Cnidus

Rhodes   Patara   Myra

CYPRUS

CRETE

Paphos   Salamis
Amathus

ANTIOCH

SYRIA

MEDITERRANEAN   SEA

Sidon   Damascus
Tyre
Ptolemais

Cyrene

Caesarea

JERUSALEM

Alexandria

JUDAEA

Petra

EGYPT

ARABIA

NILE RIVER

Mount Sinai

RED SEA

The map above attempts to trace Paul's trips throughout the eastern Mediterranean, into Asia Minor and Greece, and finally to Rome. All three missionary journeys began at Antioch, and the first two ended there. At the end of the third journey Paul was seized at Jerusalem, imprisoned, and later sent to Rome. During his travels Paul wrote letters to Christian communities he had established. At left, in an engraving from a fifteenth-century German Bible, Paul gives a messenger his Epistle to the Romans.

93

sect within the older faith. It would thus become difficult to attract gentile converts, and most probably the belief in Jesus as the Messiah would be short-lived.

For Christianity to survive, Paul realized, it had to be defined as a religion distinct from Judaism. God's will for man, the Jews had always held, involved only obedience to the law. Paul now proclaimed that belief in the death and Resurrection of Jesus was necessary for man's salvation and for the fulfillment of God's design for him. "There is neither Jew nor Greek," he said, "there is neither slave nor free, there is neither male nor female; for you are all one in Christ Jesus."

The result of these disputes was an uneasy compromise, which was reached at a conference in Jerusalem in the year 49. Paul was named Apostle to the Gentiles; and Peter, Apostle to the Jews. Many Jewish Christians continued to disagree with Paul's stand. There was no immediate solution to the problem; slowly, however, Paul's view came to prevail throughout the Christian community with both gentile and Jewish members of the new faith.

The paved road opposite, one of a vast network of highways built by the Romans in the eastern Mediterranean, was probably traveled by the Apostle Paul on his visits to Caesarea. In the fifteenth-century Spanish alabaster relief at right, Paul teaches the lessons of Jesus' life to an absorbed audience.

As missionary to the gentiles, Paul embarked on voyage after voyage to visit churches that he helped establish all over Asia Minor and Greece. Moreover, he continued to argue with the Jewish teachers in their synagogues at every stop he made. At first his headquarters was in Antioch, but it was then transferred to Ephesus on the west coast of Asia Minor, across the Aegean Sea from Athens. He visited the island of Cyprus and many other cities of Asia Minor. He journeyed over land and sea to Macedonia, where he established a church at Thessalonica, gaining his livelihood by weaving and tentmaking. He went to Athens and then to Corinth, the great maritime center of Greece. Everywhere Paul went he made converts and founded churches that continued to flourish long after he had moved on to work in other cities. Indeed, most of the congregations he organized are still in existence today. As he traveled on to new cities, Paul wrote letters to the churches he had left behind in order to guide and encourage those he had converted. These letters—or Epistles—to the Thessalonians, the Corinthians, the Ephesians, and others were eventually collected to form part of the New Testament.

Everywhere Paul traveled he met with strong opposition, particularly from Jews who resented his going into the synagogues to make converts for the new faith. His visit to Thessalonica ended with his expulsion from the town by the outraged Jews. But opposition rarely kept him from preaching in synagogues and market places and even in private homes.

To the men and women who heard him preach, Paul offered hope. His listeners were often poor. Many of them were artisans who labored in the shops that made and sold leather and textile goods, pottery and wood; or they were slaves, living in abject poverty. Like the Jews of Palestine, these people were eager for change, for their lives were intolerable in many ways. Paul came before them, bearded and with flashing eyes, his hands the rough hands of workingmen like themselves. When he promised they could have a blissful eternal life after death through faith in Jesus, most of them listened a while, shrugged their shoulders, and walked away scoffing. But some were moved by Paul's powerful preaching and came to attend services at his lodg-

At the time of Paul's visit to Corinth (ruins opposite) the Greek port was under Roman control. Known for its wealth and luxury, Corinth was also infamous as a city of vice. Paul nevertheless established a church there.

ings or at some other Christian's house. Many joined in eating the communal meals of bread and wine to commemorate the Last Supper and the death of Jesus.

Others who listened to Paul preaching in the market place—his brow furrowed and his arms waving as he talked—were puzzled. Paul was but one of many advocates of faiths that promised eternal life. Some spoke on behalf of the Persian god Mithras, promising an exalted immortality to those who joined the cult. Priests from Egypt came to Rome, claiming that the devotees of the mysterious religion of the goddess Isis would live happily forever, and the missionaries of the Greek goddess Demeter also promised a better life after death. Near Athens, at Eleusis, there was a cave, sacred to Demeter, where her worshipers congregated

An important concept of early Christianity held that Jesus as the Messiah had given a new law to supersede the law of Moses. This relief from a fourth-century sarcophagus shows Jesus (center) handing his law to Peter (right), who, like Moses,

to practice secret rites and be initiated into the goddess'
mysteries. The mysteries of Eleusis have never been revealed, for worshipers were sworn to secrecy. It is believed
that the followers of Demeter walked around a chamber, or
around the cave, as if they were making a journey to the
land of the dead. Then they "returned" safely, thanks to
their trust in the goddess.

In some ways this was similar to what Paul was preaching. Believe, he said, in this god—or Son of God—Jesus,
believe in this miracle—his Resurrection—and death will
be conquered. But Paul did more. He encouraged people to
be good through the imitation of Jesus' blameless life; and
he promised a mystical union with God through Jesus.
"The trumpet will sound," Paul wrote in his first Epistle

would carry it to the people. Occupying the other place of honor, at Jesus' right, is
Paul. At far left, Abraham is about to sacrifice his son Isaac, an Old Testament
parallel to God's sacrifice of His son, Jesus. Christ before Pilate is at far right.

to the Corinthians, "and the dead will be raised imperishable. . . . then shall come to pass the saying that is written: 'Death is swallowed up in victory.'" Few people want to die, and a religion like Christianity, which promised forgiveness of sin, salvation, and eternal life, was able to gain converts throughout the Roman Empire.

About the year 57, Paul returned to Jerusalem for a visit. Once again he was worried about his reception there, for he had never completely resolved his quarrel with the Jerusalem Christians. He suspected that they might refuse to accept him as a leader of the church. Many of his closest followers urged him to keep away from the city, but Paul insisted on going, and when he arrived, he discovered that his fears had been completely unnecessary. The Christians in the city welcomed him warmly.

However, the Jews of Jerusalem did not. Reports had reached them of the divisions he had been causing in synagogues abroad. To demonstrate that he was still loyal to the Jewish faith, Paul entered the Temple one day. When his enemies saw him there, they accused him of bringing a gentile, a Christian named Trophimus, into the Temple too, despite the prohibition against gentiles entering the inner Temple court. Paul's enemies began a riot, and the Roman garrison stationed in the tower of Antonia, overlooking the outer court, quickly came down to stop them and to arrest the troublemaker—Paul.

Once more Paul was in mortal danger. This time he was brought before the Sanhedrin for judgment, as he himself had in the past brought people, and for the same cause. When he came before the court, he claimed to be innocent of any misdemeanor. "Brethren," he said to his judges, "I have lived before God in all good conscience up to this day." Paul was a Roman citizen, and he announced to the court that he had the right to be judged for any transgression by the Roman authorities rather than by the Jews. So he was taken to Caesarea to the Roman procurator—or governor—Felix. Evidently Felix agreed with Paul's accusers, for he put him in prison at Caesarea and kept him in custody there for two years.

The confinement was not too burdensome. Paul was allowed to remain in contact with his fellow Christians, and

Caesarea (photograph opposite) includes ruined buildings from the Turkish period. During Paul's confinement there, the city was the headquarters of the Roman troops in Palestine and the residence of the Roman procurators.

when a new procurator, Festus, came into office, the Apostle was even allowed to go to Rome to plead for his freedom before the emperor.

This voyage was different from the ones he had undertaken in the past. Now he was a prisoner under the guard of a centurion and comforted only by the company of a few devout fellow Christians who had remained with him throughout his travels. The journey was uneventful until they passed Crete. Then a fierce winter storm broke out and drove the ship, with its sails furled, off its course for two weeks. The sailors panicked and threw the cargo overboard to lighten the ship. The next day, when things got no better, they threw the ship's tackle over too. Finally, they sighted land, but they had no idea what country it was.

Seeing a bay with a beach upon which they could land, the sailors attempted to maneuver toward it. The sails were unfurled to let the wind carry the ship to the shore. As luck would have it, there was a shoal directly in line, and the boat ran aground. The only way to get ashore at that point was by swimming, aided if possible by planks from the stern of the ship, which was rapidly breaking up in the heavy surf. The ship's soldiers were afraid of unloosing Paul and the other prisoners being taken to Rome, and they decided to kill them rather than let them escape. After the prisoners were killed, the others aboard would swim for their lives. But the centurion guarding Paul refused to let them kill the Apostle and forced the soldiers to change their minds. Paul, along with the others, swimming and clinging to planks from the wrecked vessel, at last reached shore.

When they reached shore, they discovered the land was Malta, a small island south of Sicily. Paul and his companions remained there for three months, preaching and trying to gain converts, until a ship that was heading for Italy came by. It was not until the spring of the year A.D. 60 that Paul finally arrived at his destination.

In Rome, while waiting for trial, Paul lived for two years under house arrest. He wore chains but probably was still able to work at his trade of tentmaking to support himself. Although the Apostle was not allowed to preach in public, he was still free to talk with his many visitors, and during this period he continued to make new converts.

A solemn but kindly looking Paul (opposite) raises his hand in a traditional gesture of blessing. The Sicilian mosaic dates from the twelfth century.

The tenth-century codex illustration at left depicts an incident described in the Acts of the Apostles: a group of Athenians mock Paul's words concerning the Resurrection of Jesus. Opposite, on a fourth-century Roman sarcophagus, Paul is taken away to his death.

The events of Paul's final years are unknown. The Apostle's dispute with the Jews may never have reached the court in Rome, and he may have remained in prison until his death. There is a tradition, however, that Paul was set free to resume his missionary journeys. He may have returned to Asia Minor or even have gone to Spain. At any rate, he was in Rome in the year 64.

That year a fire broke out and destroyed almost a quarter of the city. Terrified at the great calamity, the Romans made offerings to all of the gods and to the spirits of the underworld, hoping to avert further disasters. From the refugees who were trying to pick what was left of their few meager possessions out of the ashes came a rumor that soon swept through the entire city. It was said that the Emperor Nero, a cruel and probably insane man, had

The two great teachers of Jesus' word died for their belief—Peter (top) on the cross, and Paul (bottom) by the sword. Their martyrdom is shown here in an illustration from a tenth-century gradual, a book of psalms used in the mass.

started the fire himself to make room for new palaces and temples. A report of the tale reached Nero. To counter it, he started another rumor, accusing Rome's Christians of responsibility for starting the fire. After all, he reasoned, they had been going about the streets preaching that Rome would burn some day, along with the rest of the world, when the Messiah returned to earth.

Nero had his soldiers arrest as many Christians as they could find. The tortures inflicted on them were horrible—so horrible that the Romans, who were accustomed to seeing cruel punishments, decided that the emperor really was mad and that the Christians actually were innocent. Some victims were burned alive, a punishment Nero considered suitable for incendiaries. Some were sewn into the skins of animals and attacked by dogs, and others were run over by the emperor in his own chariot. Still others were crucified, and some women were put to death by being tied to wild bulls that were then let loose in the arena.

According to tradition, one of the victims was Paul. A second was Peter, who had also reached the city some years earlier. Paul was beheaded in a field outside Rome, alongside the road that goes toward the sea. Peter was crucified—upside down, at his own request, because he did not consider himself worthy of suffering the same death as Jesus—on Vatican Hill, across the Tiber River from the center of Rome. The little community of Christians hid in cellars or sought refuge in other cities. For safety's sake some even denied their religion and claimed to be pagans.

But in a year or two, when the danger was over, they slowly began to emerge from their hideouts and to meet again in their humble houses for the ceremony of eating bread and drinking wine in commemoration of Jesus' Last Supper. Many had died, and there were now very few left who had actually witnessed the strange events that had taken place in Palestine more than thirty years earlier or had actually heard Jesus talk and seen him die on the cross. The small community of Christians feared that their story might soon be forgotten, that the words of Jesus and his Apostles might die. To keep that from happening, a devout young man named Mark, who had probably traveled with Peter and with Paul and had heard both of them preach, began to write down the story of Jesus. His book—the Gospel according to Mark—was the first of the four Gospels and, along with Paul's Epistles, became the foundation of the New Testament.

In A.D. 68, four years after his cruel persecution of the Christians, Nero—looking vicious in this bronze bust—died by his own hand.

THE FOUR EVANGELISTS

During the early centuries of Christianity, many works concerning the life and teachings of Jesus were written. In A.D. 367 Bishop Athanasius of Alexandria first proposed the list of twenty-seven books contained in today's New Testament. Not until the end of the fifth century, however, was this list officially adopted by the Church. Other works were labeled apocryphal, or of unknown origin and doubtful authenticity. Most important perhaps of the accepted works are the four Gospels (from the Anglo-Saxon word for good tidings) of Matthew, Mark, Luke, and John. The four Evangelists are shown opposite in a twelfth-century Coptic manuscript illustration. The Gospel of Mark, believed to be the oldest written record of Jesus, is traditionally attributed to Mark, a disciple and companion of both Peter and Paul. The Gospels of Matthew and Luke are apparently based on Mark, although each of the two contain added incidents and more of Jesus' teaching. Because of their similarities, the first three works are known as the Synoptic Gospels (from the Greek word *synopsis*, "seeing together"). The anonymous author of Matthew's Gospel is thought to have based his work on the teachings of the Apostle Matthew; Luke is supposed to have been a physician, a gentile convert, and a friend of Paul's. The last of the Gospels, that of John, was long thought to have been composed by a follower of the Apostle John, traditionally considered the youngest and most devoted of Jesus' Disciples. In a vision of the Old Testament prophet Ezekiel, four living creatures appear. Each has the face of a man on one side of his head, but the likenesses of a lion, an ox, and an eagle on the other three sides. The New Testament Book of Revelation, attributed to the author of John's Gospel, tells of another vision in which four beings stand at the throne of God. One has the face of a man; the others, features of the three creatures described by Ezekiel. In time these symbols were applied to the Evangelists. Matthew, who stressed Jesus as the embodiment of ancient prophecies, became a winged man; Mark, who wrote for Christian martyrs in Rome, was represented as a lion; Luke, who emphasized Jesus' death and Resurrection, was shown as a sacrificial ox; and John became an eagle, for his soaring inspiration. The traditional symbols, for which various explanations have been given, are shown above, on either side of Jesus, in an eighth-century English miniature.

VI

JERUSALEM BESIEGED

During the years in which Paul was traveling about the Mediterranean world seeking converts to Christianity, the Jews of Palestine were coming closer to the breaking point under Roman oppression. Most of the Roman procurators who governed the country were interested only in making fortunes—in squeezing what wealth they could from their subjects before their terms of office expired. Riots broke out often, and in several cities, but they were quickly suppressed. Taking advantage of the unrest, gentiles in Palestine tried to deprive the Jews of their rights under Roman law and to usurp their power in the land. The Roman soldiers were more interested in plundering the Jews than in protecting them; and whenever anyone showed signs of discontent, the Romans threw him into prison.

In the city of Jerusalem, a group of patriots—the Sicarii, or "dagger men"—roamed through the streets, assassinating Romans and any Jews they suspected of being friendly to the Roman cause. The Romans captured and imprisoned many of them, but the procurator, Festus—the man who had ordered Paul to Rome to stand trial—was so greedy for money that he allowed some Sicarii to be ransomed by their relatives. In order to pay Festus, the other Sicarii attacked and robbed the rich. They handed the money over to Festus, and the imprisoned assassins were set free to continue their crimes until they were caught again.

At the time, various wandering prophets were urging the people to march into the desert to await a sign from God, a sign that would mark the beginning of the great rebellion against Rome. One of these prophets led hundreds of people to the top of the Mount of Olives overlooking

The fierce Roman infantry opposite, wearing armor and carrying javelins and shields, adorns the second-century Column of Marcus Aurelius in Rome. The city's invincible legionaries conquered nations from Britain to Palestine.

Jerusalem's houses appear as an oval cluster left of center in this fifth-century mosaic map of Palestine from the Madeba

basilica in Jordan. Above the missing central section are boats in the Mediterranean. Place names are in Greek.

Jerusalem. They planned to capture the city, put the Roman garrison to death, and inaugurate the kingdom of God. The authorities dealt with this threat as harshly as they had with John the Baptist, Jesus, and Theudas. Roman troops quickly routed the rebels from the Mount of Olives, slaughtering those who did not escape and capturing and executing most of the leaders.

Over the years, Roman disregard of Jewish religious feeling had become more open; Roman taxes had become more burdensome; and the poverty of the people had become more acute. In the year 64, the Temple, which Herod had begun rebuilding a century earlier, was finally completed, down to the last bit of carving on the marble façade. It was a beautiful and noble building of which the Jews were extremely proud—especially since Herod was long dead. But its completion threw thousands of men out of jobs, and the government had to set up a work project for the unemployed. In order to keep the jobless from starving, the authorities put them to work repaving all the streets of Jerusalem with marble left over from the Temple construction. These jobs reduced the want of some, but throughout the country thousands continued to go hungry. It seemed evident now that rebellion, which had been seething for decades, would soon break out in the Holy Land.

In the spring of 66, the new procurator, Florus, made the mistake of requisitioning a great quantity of gold belonging to the Temple, and the revolt finally erupted. The Jews were outraged at this violation of their religious center. So scornful of Roman greed were some of them that a group of young men paraded about the streets of Jerusalem with baskets, pretending to be taking up a collection to help poor Florus. The procurator was so enraged by their insolence that he marched a Roman army up to Jerusalem from his capital at Caesarea. The troops seized and slaughtered—many by crucifixion—some thirty-six hundred rebellious Jews.

Roman oppression had at last gone too far. The angry people of Jerusalem stormed through the streets, burning the house of the High Priest, who favored the Roman cause, and some of the palaces that Herod had constructed in the city. They sacked the official archives, and as cheering crowds looked on, burned all records of indebtedness to the rich, thus freeing the poor from financial oppression. A contingent of men was sent across the desert to Masada, where they raided the armory and seized spears, shields, and arrows. Returning to Jerusalem, they broke into the

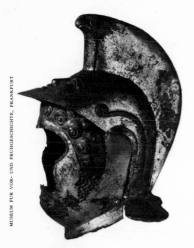

The faceplate of this bronze Roman parade helmet is decorated in relief with a beard and forelocks.

The rolling hill country of Galilee, tranquil in this modern photograph of the western shore of the Sea of Galilee, seethed with rebellion against Rome in the first century.

Temple and killed the High Priest. The rebels were complete masters of the city.

The revolt was led by the Zealots, the extreme branch of the Pharisees that had long advocated open rebellion against the foreign oppressors. They were resolved to expel the Romans from the Holy Land and re-establish an independent Jewish nation ruled by God alone and governed in accordance with Jewish religious law.

For four years the Jerusalem rebels succeeded in holding their own against the best armies Rome could muster. Florus' force was not strong enough to take the city. He had to withdraw and try to wipe out resistance in the rest of the country, for rebellion had broken out not only in Jerusalem but throughout the Holy Land. The population of Galilee was especially determined to expel the Romans. But the imperial troops entered the province in strength, burning villages and fields and killing or selling into slavery men who were capable of bearing arms.

Roman strategy was slow and deliberate. The Romans preferred to wait and build up their forces, bottle up the Jewish armies in various cities, and then besiege them until they surrendered. But often they found that the Jews did not surrender; they preferred to die fighting. Yet, in battle after battle, in siege after siege, the relentless Roman war machine slowly gained control of the country. By A.D. 68, Galilee had been completely subdued; by the spring of the following year, the entire country outside Jerusalem had been reconquered.

During these years, while war raged throughout the rest of the country, the Holy City had remained free, its strong fortifications defying every attempt by the Romans to conquer it. As the outlying districts were slowly brought under

Under the empire, Romans added cavalry to their vast armies. In the relief detail opposite, cavalrymen, some dismounted, skirmish with an enemy. On the march, Roman legionaries carried their personal armor and weapons, but heavy equipment was pulled by mule-drawn carts (left). The two scenes are from the Column of Marcus Aurelius.

Roman control, refugees fled into the city. Some were fierce Zealots from Galilee who were prepared to fight to the finish; others were country people who desired only peace after having seen their farms and estates burned by the foraging Roman troops. Still other refugees were members of devout religious communities who refused to live under Roman rule. The Essenes were driven from their settlement at Qumran, and the abandoned community lay forgotten in the wilderness for nineteen centuries.

Pilgrims to the Temple swelled the population of the already crowded city. The small community of Jerusalem Christians, however, fled to Pella, twenty miles south of the Sea of Galilee. They were not interested in the rebellion against the Romans. Their only concern was waiting patiently for an event their leaders had predicted would happen soon: the Second Coming, Jesus' return to earth in glory as the Messiah.

It was dangerous to walk about at night in Jerusalem. The Sicarii still made a practice of assassinating anyone

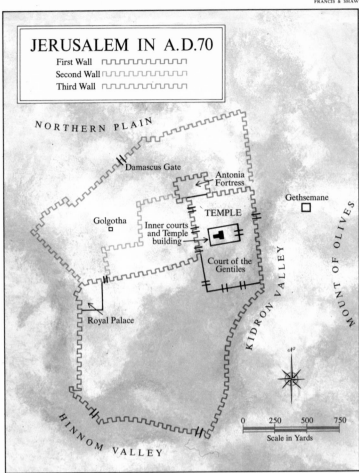

JERUSALEM IN A.D. 70

First Wall ᴧᴧᴧᴧᴧᴧᴧᴧᴧᴧ
Second Wall ᴧᴧᴧᴧᴧᴧᴧᴧᴧᴧ
Third Wall ᴧᴧᴧᴧᴧᴧᴧᴧᴧᴧ

NORTHERN PLAIN

Damascus Gate

Antonia Fortress

Gethsemane

Golgotha

TEMPLE

Inner courts and Temple building

Court of the Gentiles

Royal Palace

KIDRON VALLEY

MOUNT OF OLIVES

HINNOM VALLEY

0   250   500   750
Scale in Yards

The map of Jerusalem at right defines the system of walls that divided the Holy City into separate defense sectors. Only a single wall rose above the valleys that protected the city on three sides, while three successive walls faced the northern plain, the inviting attack route taken by the Roman general Titus in A.D. 70. Golgotha, scene of Jesus' crucifixion, was by this time within the city walls.

whom they suspected of wanting to make peace. To add to this menace, a fierce civil war raged among three bands of Zealots who were all determined to win the war but disagreed on how to do it. One group—with their cry "No king but God"—seized the Temple and used it as a fortress. They continued to perform the Temple sacrifices, even while under attack from a rival band, which was itself being assaulted by soldiers of the third Zealot group. The Zealots were so full of hatred for one another that they seemed to have lost their senses. Members of the three groups even burned one another's food supplies.

When the Romans received reports of this internal strife, they thought that the Jews in Jerusalem would be easy to conquer. In the spring of the year A.D. 70, the Roman commander Titus ordered his forces up to the city and began to surround it. He set up his headquarters on Mount Scopus, northeast of Jerusalem, and built camps for his troops around the city walls. Only when the Roman armies came into sight did the Jewish factions decide that it was time to compose their differences and prepare for the siege.

On three sides Jerusalem was protected by steep ravines that made it almost impossible for any attacking force to approach. It was even dangerous for an enemy to station troops right outside the city, for soldiers in the ravine below were easy marks for Jewish defenders standing on the walls. But on one side, the north side of the city, there is a plain, and overlooking it a range of higher hills. It was from there that any attack would come; it was from there that conquerors in the past had usually managed to make their way into the city.

To guard this one vulnerable approach, the city was fortified with three walls on the northern side. The contemporary Jewish historian Josephus—no doubt to make his story more dramatic—assigned huge dimensions and numbers to the walls and their towers. The outer wall, he wrote, was thirty feet high and fifteen feet thick and was surmounted by ninety towers spaced at 300-foot intervals. The middle wall had forty towers; the inner, sixty. One of the outer towers stood an incredible 105 feet, about as high as a ten-story building. From the top of the towers, Josephus wrote, one could see—some thirty-five miles away—the Mediterranean Sea. These walls divided Jerusalem into sections and made it possible for the defenders to hold out in one part of the city long after another part was taken. Moreover, Jerusalem itself was a mass of narrow alleys in which guerrillas could cut an invading enemy to pieces.

Around the circumference of the city—which perhaps extended more than four miles—there were several gates. At each, the walls had been widened. The gate houses were actually large rooms, and there were several places at which they could be closed to keep out unwelcome visitors. The Temple mount, one of the highest parts of the city, could be closed off behind its own walls, and various palaces and towers inside the town could also be defended independently. Its natural situation and its defenses made Jerusalem one of the great fortresses of the ancient world. The Romans were well aware of its strength. Indeed, some of the imperial troops came to believe—as the Jews did— that the city was divinely protected and thus impregnable. A few Romans even deserted to the Jewish side.

From his camp on Mount Scopus, overlooking the vulnerable side of Jerusalem, Titus made his plans for the cap-

The profile of Titus, who reigned as emperor for two years, appears on this first-century gold coin.

OVERLEAF: *The classic method of siege warfare, by which Jerusalem was conquered, is depicted in an eleventh-century manuscript illustration. Heavily armed troops attack a city from four sides as apprehensive citizens watch. The artist is in the picture, at lower right.*

119

ture of the Holy City. Accompanied by only a small guard, he rode around the walls of the city to find the most effective way to attack it. As he came within shooting distance of the walls, the Jews let loose a volley of arrows. One of his men was hit, but Titus and the rest of the troop galloped off to safety.

When he got back to camp, Titus ordered his men to sweep through the outskirts of the city, destroying whatever they could. He ordered all trees in the neighborhood cut down to make war engines. His men did their work thoroughly; a wide and desolate no man's land soon surrounded the city. It is only in the present century that trees have begun to grow there again. Siege engines were constructed, and the tallest and strongest timbers were chosen to make battering rams. Catapults began to bombard the defenders with stones, the one war material that was plentiful in the region, for the Judaean hills are covered with rocks.

The Jews attempted to set fire to the Roman equipment by throwing firebrands from their vantage points, and some even leaped down to dismantle the siege engines. But the enemy was too vigilant, and the Romans managed to win most of these pitched battles with the Jewish forces. By the fifteenth day of the siege, the battering rams had done their work. A break appeared in the outer wall, and the Romans poured through the gap. The Jews were forced to withdraw into the heart of the city, behind the second wall.

Five days later, the Romans succeeded in breaching the second wall. Led by Titus, the legionaries rushed into the narrow streets and alleys of a section containing the wool market and the shops of the clothes dealers and workers in brass. But in this labyrinth, the Romans were quickly separated from one another. They had failed to widen the break in the wall behind them, and when the Jews attacked they had difficulty retreating. Titus managed to escape, but many of his men were surrounded and killed. The Jews quickly moved to repair the breach in the wall. Four days later, however, Titus completed his destruction of the second wall. The Jews now had only their innermost defense line.

At this point Titus decided that the best thing to do was to destroy the morale of the Jews rather than continue his costly assaults. The Jews within their defenses grew uneasy at the unaccustomed silence, wondering what new strategy the Romans were planning. They soon saw the answer. Within full view of the defenders of the city, but just outside

Roman legionaries, professional builders as well as soldiers, construct fortifications in this relief detail from Trajan's column.

the range of Jewish arrows, Titus' men placed two great piles of silver and gold coins on the ground. The people within the city had never seen anything like it; thousands of them rushed to the walls to see what would happen. With great pomp, the Roman army marched in review past its commander—four legions of fully armed infantry, cavalry, and other auxiliary troops, possibly as many as 30,000 men. As each man marched by, he was paid his salary from the great heaps of silver and gold at Titus' side. The parade took four full days. Seeing the enormous and perfectly trained army assembled against them, the Jews were filled with foreboding.

Inside the walls there were about eighty thousand people, one fourth of them fighting men. Originally there had been more defenders, but many had already been killed, and, in the first weeks of the siege, several thousand Jews had managed to flee past the Roman lines. Titus had meanwhile kept urging the Jews to surrender, to spare themselves the rigor of a siege and keep their Holy City and Temple safe. At first, many of them accepted this offer of amnesty. But when they discovered that the Roman soldiers were slitting open some of the refugees to see if they had smuggled treasure out by swallowing pieces of gold, the Jews decided that it was better to stay in Jerusalem and risk starvation. As the weeks went by, the famine in the besieged town grew worse and worse. The people became so hungry that they gnawed the leather of their belts and sandals for food; one woman, it was said, was so crazed by hunger that she even devoured her own child. Early in the siege some Jews managed to sneak outside the walls to forage for food in the ravines beneath the city. But the Romans began rounding up all of the foragers they could find and crucifying them—often as many as five hundred a day —in full view of the city's populace. Whenever they captured a Jewish soldier, they cut off one of his hands and sent him back into the city to urge the defenders to surrender. Without a hand, the soldier could no longer fight against the Romans, and yet he would still consume a portion of the precious food supply.

Within the crowded little houses people began to mutter that there was no possibility of relief. In the southern quarters of the city, the oldest part, the inhabitants began to suffer from the stench of the dead bodies that had been thrown over the nearby wall to rot in the ravine below. The starving people could climb up on the walls and see, not far away, the Roman camp, where food was plentiful. Within the city there seemed to be nothing but desolation and death; outside there seemed to be hope. Some people tried to escape, but the leaders of the revolt announced that no one would be allowed to leave. It was better, they said, to die fighting in defense of Jewish freedom—as God willed—than surrender to Rome. And, despite their suffering, most of the population refused to think of compromise. They remembered the many stories in the Bible of miracles that had in the past saved the Jews from their enemies, and they expected that now too a miracle would save them. The Messiah would surely come in the midst of their affliction and turn what seemed to be a defeat into a victory.

One of the city's famous scholars, who devoted his days to the study and teaching of the Torah, was less optimistic. Jochanan ben Zakkai, the most respected scholar of his day, was an old man when the siege began. Opposed to war with Rome, Jochanan felt that even under Rome the Jews could continue their existence with some freedom. It was best, he thought, to suffer Roman oppression patiently and wait for a change.

Jochanan had little expectation that the Messiah would come immediately to save the people from their troubles. "If you are planting a tree and someone should come along and tell you that the Messiah has arrived, don't drop everything and run," he would say. "Finish planting the tree first."

Throughout the war, Jochanan had continued teaching at his school within the porticoes of the Temple. Young and old alike came to learn from him, as Paul had once gone to Gamaliel, Jochanan's own teacher, more than thirty years earlier. But, as the siege lengthened, it became evident to him that the defenders of Jerusalem had no chance at all of saving the Holy City. When the Romans won, he reasoned, all of the inhabitants would be killed or enslaved. At last Jochanan decided to flee—to Roman protection—not to save his own life but rather to save his people. For he knew that when Jerusalem fell, its great academies would perish with it. If the academies were to vanish, then the great tradition of Jewish learning, which kept the teachings of the Bible alive, would also perish.

Jochanan was determined to keep this from happening. He felt that only by leaving the city and re-establishing his school elsewhere could he make sure it would survive. But how would he be able to flee the city when the leaders of the rebellion had warned the population that any person who attempted to escape from Jerusalem would be killed?

The imperial eagle, the symbol of Roman power first carried on legion standards, decorates the face of this first-century B.C. onyx cameo.

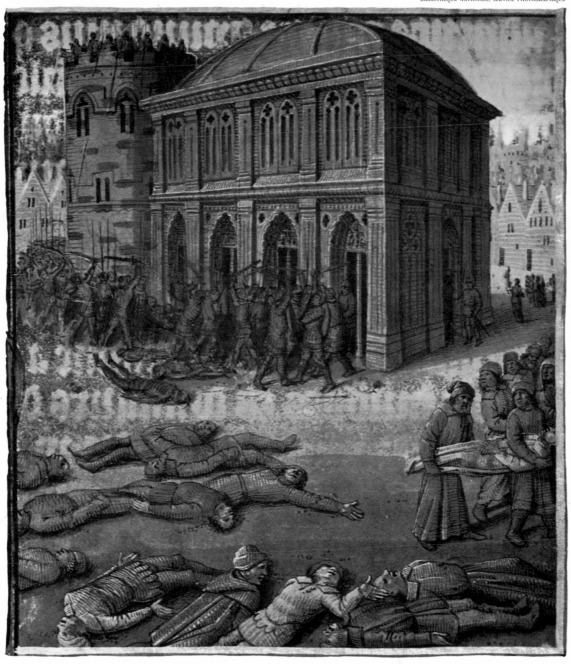

Hand-to-hand fighting around the Jerusalem Temple followed the Roman break-through into the plague-ridden city. One shroud-covered victim is carried away (right); others lie unburied (foreground). This illustration by Fouquet, like those on pages 10 and 24, is for a fifteenth-century manuscript of Josephus' Antiquities of the Jews.

With a few of his disciples, he hit upon a plan. He would pretend to be sick and to die, and his students would carry him outside for burial. Then, once beyond the walls, he would go to the Romans and beg for a safe conduct to pass through the siege lines. In order to prepare for his "funeral," Jochanan kept himself away from his school for a few days, pretending to be ill. Only his favored pupils, who were in on the secret, were allowed to attend the aged scholar. While he was at home he practiced lying perfectly still, breathing as quietly and with as little motion as possible. Finally the day came when his disciples, tears in their eyes, went to the Temple to announce that Jochanan was dead and that this same day he would be carried outside the walls to be buried. They wrapped him in his funeral shroud, the long, simple white robe that Jews are traditionally buried in, rich and poor alike, so that there will be no distinction among them after death. Then Jochanan's students placed a small piece of meat—a rare commodity during the siege—beneath the shroud so that the corpse would seem to smell. Carrying the bier, the few planks on which the body rested, his disciples went to the gates of the city to take Jochanan outside.

The soldiers on guard were suspicious. Why should this corpse be carried outside for burial when other bodies were just thrown over the wall? Upon discovering that the body was that of a distinguished scholar, the soldiers decided that Jochanan deserved a proper burial, and they permitted the procession to pass.

As soon as he reached safety, Jochanan took the shroud from his face and stood up. He and his disciples made their way to the Roman camp where the Roman leaders welcomed them eagerly. They were happy to have so important a man come over to their side to seek refuge.

But Jochanan was not interested in merely seeking refuge. What he wanted was to re-establish his school, and he told the Romans that all he wanted from them was permission to go to a quiet and peaceful town to begin his work all over again. They decided to grant his request. It was to their advantage now to be as cooperative as possible, for if word got back to the defenders of Jerusalem that the Romans were generous in victory, then the citizens might be tempted to surrender. Jochanan went off in peace to Yavneh, a small town a few miles south of the modern city of Tel Aviv, where before long he began to gather a few students around him. In Jerusalem, however, the siege continued, for the Romans' diplomatic treatment of Jochanan did not tempt the city's defenders to surrender.

The Romans began to build great mounds of earth and stone opposite Jerusalem's final wall of defense so that soldiers on top of the earthworks could assault the Jews from an equal or higher level. This was dangerous work, for the builders were constantly under a hail of arrows and stones from the old wall, even when they were protected by covering fire from their own troops. But slowly the ramps took shape. Finally, after several weeks, the Romans, from their newly constructed position, were able to attack the wall adjoining one of the city's strongest fortresses, the Antonia, which Herod had built years before and named after his protector Marc Antony. At night the Romans stole into the fort and overpowered the guards. When the Jews heard them come in, however, they roused the entire defending army and joined in a desperate battle to expel the enemy. Because the range was too close for Roman catapults to be used, legionaries fought ferociously in hand-to-hand combat with the Jews, slashing with their swords and trampling on the fallen until the streets were deep in dead bodies. The attack was so fierce that the Jewish soldiers were forced to retreat to the Temple enclosure. Thousands of people fled in terror with them and huddled on the vast terrace, impeding the movement of the defending troops. Meanwhile, the Romans had gained possession of the Antonia fortress, which towered over the Temple site.

Finally, in late summer, five months after the siege of the city had begun, the Romans succeeded in breaching the

An illustration from Meir Yaffe's fifteenth-century Haggada conveys the isolation of the enslaved Jews: a lonely survivor chops wood for his master.

outer Temple walls by setting fire to the gates. The Jews retreated behind the walls of the inner court but were able to hold out there for only one more day. Their final retreat, into the Temple building itself, gave them still another day's refuge.

For some time now the daily Temple sacrifice had no longer been offered. It was far better, the Jews decided, to eat the sacrificial animals and drink the wine in the Temple storerooms in order to keep alive. When the Romans came through the Temple walls, the Jews there were too weakened by hunger and by the effects of the long siege to defend themselves well. Wherever they lay they were mercilessly slaughtered—infants and old people, women and children —thousands in all. The Romans rushed eagerly into the Temple buildings to find the fabulous treasure they had heard was hidden there; but no treasure was to be found. Titus himself followed his troops into the Temple and walked into the Holy of Holies to inspect the famous sanctuary and to see for himself the notorious shrine that contained no image of a god. His men were furious that they had found no treasure. One of them threw a torch, and the soldiers cheered as they saw the walls catch fire. As Titus walked out of the burning building he saw his soldiers setting fire to other parts of the Temple. He did not stop them.

Within the Temple enclosure a few Jews in isolated spots continued to fight on against overwhelming odds. Most were killed, but a few were captured. Among the captives, many refused to acknowledge that the Roman emperor was their sovereign. Even under torture they refused to call any man "Lord"; they owed allegiance, they insisted, only to God. Atop one of the Temple colonnades, far above the fighting, many women and children had sought refuge. The Romans set this colonnade on fire, and those refugees who were not burned to death perished when they jumped off to escape the flames. The Roman soldiers carried their ensigns into the Temple—eagles atop great poles, with the number of the legion engraved beneath, and they sacrificed to them, a pagan sacrifice to pagan gods on the site of the Temple of the Jews.

Inside the city, a few Jews still held out against the Romans, and they took the opportunity, while the Roman soldiers were preoccupied with capturing the Temple, to break through the Roman lines and flee into the desert. Behind them they could see the city covered with flames from the burning Temple and from the fires that Titus had ordered the Romans to set all over Jerusalem, destroying

His hands bound, a defeated enemy is led away by a Roman legionary.

the Holy City of the Jews as a warning to them never to rebel again.

The people who remained in the ruined city were herded together. The tallest and handsomest youths were saved to march in chains through the streets of Rome in Titus' triumph, to show the Romans what a powerful enemy Titus had conquered. The old and infirm were slain, while those judged able to survive were taken to a stockade the Romans set up amid the ruins of the Temple. Although there was now food in plenty, the Romans were not generous in handing it out to the prisoners, and thousands starved to death. The survivors were put in chains and sent into Egypt to spend the rest of their lives in misery, working there as slaves just as their ancestors in Moses' time had once done. A few were kept aside to be sent off to arenas throughout the Roman Empire. In the arenas they would be killed in combat with gladiators or thrown to the wild beasts while audiences cheered.

The war was at an end—a war that was the most terrible the world had ever known. No war before in history had been as fiercely contested or had cost so many lives. The Romans had finally subjugated their rebellious province—most of it, anyway. "The Romans make a desert and call it peace," a king of Britain who had fought the Romans once said. A Roman peace had come to the Holy Land. It was in ruins.

The Jews had suffered one of the most crippling defeats in their long history, and it seemed as though they could never rise again. Their capital city was a heap of rubble. The Temple, around which their religion was centered, was completely destroyed. Thousands of their people had been sent into exile or slavery far from their ancient homeland. It seemed now that the Jews were about to disappear as a nation, that Rome had succeeded in destroying them, something that other enemies—the Egyptians, the Babylonians, the Assyrians, and the Greeks had tried but had never been able to do. It seemed as if two thousand years of Jewish history was at an end.

But there was still that small group of refugees who had succeeded in fleeing from the burning city of Jerusalem. Slowly they made their way through the wilderness, foraging for food wherever they could in that desolate landscape. And in the little town of Yavneh, the old scholar Jochanan gathered his students around him. Even though the Temple was gone and the nation was destroyed, they began thinking of ways to save the Jewish religion.

ROGER-VIOLLET

A coin struck during the reign of Emperor Vespasian (father of Titus) commemorates Rome's victory. The mourning Jewish nation sits beneath a tree symbolizing Judaea.

VII   STRUGGLE TO SURVIVE

With the fall of Jerusalem, the Romans decided to teach the Jews a stern lesson—one that would serve as a warning to any other subject nation that dared to rebel. Thenceforth, the Jews were to be marked as a people different from all others, deserving of punishment and required to meet special obligations. To penalize them the Romans forbade the reconstruction of the Jerusalem Temple. The tax that the Jews had previously paid voluntarily for its upkeep was now imposed on them by force; but it went not to Jerusa-

Roman troops marching in triumph through the streets of Rome exhibit spoils—including a menorah from the Temple—after Jerusalem's conquest. The detail is from the first-century Arch of Titus.

STEMATE VESTITVS PREFVLGET CVM PATRE TITVS

Josephus (far right) carrying a volume of The Jewish War *hurries along a road toward the enthroned Emperor Vespasian and his son Titus, to whom Josephus dedicated his work. Curious crowds follow the historian in this illumination from an eleventh-century Latin manuscript of Josephus' history.*

lem but to Rome, to support the pagan temples. This tax outraged their religious feelings; yet it had to be paid by all Jews throughout the Roman Empire, even those in lands and cities far from the seat of rebellion. Centuries later, long after the Roman Empire had fallen, and new societies had risen in its place, discriminatory measures such as this continued to be taken against the Jews.

To celebrate his victory, Titus built a triumphal arch in the Roman Forum. Carved on it were Jewish captives carrying their sacred Temple objects through the streets of Rome in Titus' victory procession. In the Holy Land, Jewish property was confiscated; in fact, no Jew was allowed to own land in the country. Farmers who had tilled their own small fields found themselves working as sharecroppers on the great estates of Roman landlords. Others, expelled from their homes, traveled abroad, to live in lands where

they would always be treated as foreigners. The great Jewish city of Jerusalem was in ruins, and no Jew was allowed to settle there again. Jews were permitted to visit the ruins and recite prayers at the site of the Temple, but Roman troops were stationed nearby to see that they did not linger.

For three years after the fall of Jerusalem in A.D. 70, some Jews continued to fight the Romans. In three desert citadels that had originally been fortified by Herod, bands of Zealots kept alive Jewish resistance. Slowly, the Roman troops moved south and invested them. Two of the forts—Machaerus, where John the Baptist had been killed, and Herodium, in the wilderness of Judaea near the town of Bethlehem—surrendered. But the third, Masada, held out longer.

The Zealots at Masada were led by Eleazar, who had commanded some of them during the siege of Jerusalem.

Columns of sandstone drums stand in the ruins of Masada at the edge of a cliff overlooking the Dead Sea.

When they fled the city and arrived at Masada, they found enormous stores of barley and wheat, olive oil, wine, and dates placed there a full century earlier by Herod and perfectly preserved in the dry air of the Dead Sea basin. The vast cisterns of the fort held ample supplies of water, as long as strict rationing was imposed. The fortress itself was almost impregnable. Nevertheless, the Romans were determined to assault Masada, to leave no corner of Palestine where rebellious Jews could find shelter. They built a camp at the base of the towering bluff; the ruins of this camp can still be seen. Cautiously, the Romans began forcing their way up Masada, although exposed to attacks from the defenders above.

It took the Romans almost a year to reach the top of the mountain; but finally in the spring of A.D. 73 they succeeded. Atop Masada, they built a wall around the fortress, tightening their grip on the Jews and preventing their escape. When the Romans began battering at the fortress walls, the Jews hastily erected an inner defensive line. But as soon as the Romans broke through the outer wall, they set fire to the inner one. It was evident that the Romans would now overcome the defenders, the last unconquered Jews in the Holy Land.

Still the Zealots refused to surrender. Although they knew that they could hold out no longer, they vowed to die rather than give in to the Romans. The Jewish historian Josephus describes the sad scene: "... they clasped and fondly embraced their wives and took their children in their arms, clinging to them and weeping as they kissed them for the last time." Then each man, "... as if executing [them] with a stranger's hands," killed his wife and children to keep them from being killed by the Romans or sent off to a life of slavery. Next "... they quickly heaped together all their effects and set fire to them; and ... having chosen by lot ten of their number to slay the rest, they laid themselves down, each beside his fallen wife and children, and throwing their arms around them, made ready their throats for those who discharged the mournful office."

The ten men chosen by lot cut the throats of their comrades. Then they drew lots once more to choose the man who would kill the other nine. Upon finishing his grisly task, he looked around the room at the scene of the slaughter and finally plunged his sword into his own body. All in all, 953 people had been killed.

Seven years after it had begun, the great war against the Roman Empire ended—in utter defeat for the Jews.

Out of their defeat, however, the Jews created new life. For they were determined not to disappear, as the Babylonians, the Hittites, the Phoenicians, the Etruscans, the Carthaginians, and so many other nations had disappeared when they were overwhelmed by a stronger power. Despite this disaster, and despite others they were to encounter in the years ahead, the Jews have managed to survive for centuries—even down to the present day. Although their independence, their homeland, and their Temple had been lost, there was still one thing the Jews had left: their religion, as embodied in the Torah.

It was the Torah that preserved the faith of the Jews. And the study of the Torah itself was preserved by men such as Jochanan ben Zakkai, who had smuggled himself out of the besieged city of Jerusalem to make sure that the schools of the Torah would continue. At Yavneh, to which other scholars had fled from the ravages of war, Jochanan assembled a group of his followers. They met daily in a vineyard to study the law and the traditions concerning it that had been passed down through the generations.

When news of the destruction of the Temple spread through the Holy Land, people went into mourning. Many of them supposed that the Jewish religion was also destroyed. Some Jews mourned so deeply that they refused to eat meat or drink wine until the Temple was rebuilt because these items had been used in the Temple ritual. And some even refused to bring children into a world of such unhappiness and uncertainty. Grieving the loss of the Temple, the rabbis at Yavneh decreed certain rules of mourning to be followed: women were to wear fewer jewels and cosmetics; certain prayers were to be recited; in every new house a patch of wall was to be left unpainted. But the rabbis were Pharisees, and as Pharisees they were interested in considering the present as well as the past. They proclaimed that it was wrong, even sinful, to mourn too deeply. No one should refrain from having children. After all, they pointed out, the very first command of God recorded in the Bible is "Be fruitful and multiply."

The rabbis at Yavneh, and their successors, spent a great deal of time and energy studying the Temple rituals and recording their studies for the future. It was essential, they believed, that their descendants know just how to perform the sacrifices that are commanded in the Bible when the Temple was built again, as they strongly believed it would be. They all remembered that the Temple had been destroyed once before, in 586 B.C., and then rebuilt. In the

Roman coins dating from the second and third year of the Jewish rebellion were found at Masada.

The rabbis of Yavneh carried on the traditions established in Jerusalem before the rebellion. In this illumination from a thirteenth-century Haggada, Rabbi Gamaliel instructs three disciples.

meantime, to substitute for the Temple sacrifice required of every Jew, they adopted eighteen benedictions or prayers to be recited every day. Many Jews still recite them daily.

One of these prayers asked God to "favor us with knowledge, understanding, and discernment." For to the rabbis of Yavneh, and to the Jews throughout the ages who inherited their traditions, study was one of man's most important occupations. They spent hour after hour poring over the law, arguing about its meaning and trying to find out exactly what was intended by the commandments in the Torah.

What, for instance, was meant when one of the Ten Commandments said: "Six days shall work be done, but on the seventh you shall have a holy sabbath of solemn rest to the Lord." In a way this seemed clear cut: no one should do any work on Saturday, the seventh day of the week. But did it include doctors, who might be needed to save a life on the Sabbath; or soldiers, who were needed to protect a town? Evidently not, the rabbis decided. In analyzing such problems, most of the rabbis took the position that the demands of life took precedence over any law of the Bible, for after all, the law was there to enhance life. And so they decided that if it was necessary, a doctor could work on the Sabbath, but a woodcutter or a shoemaker could not.

Soon after the school at Yavneh had been established, Jochanan ben Zakkai died, and he was succeeded as its leader by a rabbi named Gamaliel, who had been the head of the Sanhedrin in Jerusalem. Gamaliel and the scholars around him continued to collect the decisions and the debates about such problems as working on the Sabbath. They determined to establish general rules for all to follow.

Some Jews, followers of a school established by the famous rabbi Shammai, would not—to choose a minor example—leave a trap to catch a bird over the Sabbath, while the followers of the great rabbi Hillel, who had lived at the time of Jesus, would. The scholars at Yavneh decided that with the Temple destroyed and the Jews so scattered, disunity was a great danger. It was best to establish one rule of conduct for all Jews. They decided that henceforth a simple majority vote of the rabbis would be enough to establish the correct interpretation of the law. Where in the past two interpretations had been permitted side by side— as in the matter of setting hunting traps—they voted to accept the rule of Hillel and his school and rejected the strict interpretation of Shammai. In this they were favoring the majority of the people. They were also thinking of the poor,

Many traditions survived the fall of the Temple. Three illustrations from Meir Yaffe's German Haggada show offerings made on Passover: one man holds unleavened bread (top); another roasts a lamb (middle); and the last offers herbs.

who might need the food that would be caught in a trap over the Sabbath, whereas the rich would not care.

In most cases the majority favored a liberal interpretation of the law and opposed keeping only to its letter and not its spirit. For as one rabbi said, "The Sabbath is delivered in your hand, and not you in its hand," which is a thought that Jesus also expressed. The rabbis tried to base every interpretation on the principle that the purpose of all law was to make life better. Anything detrimental to life was forbidden, even though it might not be mentioned in the Torah. Thus, Jews were forbidden, for instance, to live in a town in which there was no physician. And so the majority opinion among the Pharisees came to prevail as the standard for Jews everywhere. Groups like the Essenes died out, and the Sadducees, whose influence was based on the Temple ritual, disappeared when the Temple was destroyed.

This drawing representing Jesus' multiplication of the loaves and fishes appears on the wall of a third-century Christian catacomb.

The debates and decisions of the rabbis were not written down until a century after the fall of Jerusalem. Scholars were reluctant to record them, for they were afraid that a new book might seem to compete with the Bible. And so they were passed down by word of mouth, from teacher to pupil, decade after decade. Finally, however, these traditions were assembled and set down by a great rabbi, Judah ha-Nasi, at the end of the second century. This work was called the Mishnah. Not just a collection of legal decisions and debates, the Mishnah was also a guide to enable future scholars to interpret the Torah.

For centuries thereafter, in studying the Bible, scholars were guided by the Mishnah. Their work went on both in Palestine—under later persecution by the Romans the rabbinical academy moved north from Yavneh to various towns in Galilee—and in Babylonia, where many Jews fled to live under Persian rule and away from Roman persecution. Further interpretations were compiled, both in Palestine and in Babylonia, up to about the year 400. These commentaries were called the Gemara, from another word meaning "study." The Mishnah and the Gemara together came to be known as the Talmud, and the Talmud became almost as important a guide to the Jewish religion as the Bible itself. Jews since then have been studying both the Torah and the Talmud—the law and its interpretations—and have been guided by their decrees.

Meanwhile, in the decades after the fall of Jerusalem, the Christian churches slowly gained strength. Converts came in increasing numbers to the small Christian congre-

Another Christian wall-painting of the third century portrays Jesus as the Good Shepherd tending his flock of sheep—the sheep are the symbol of his spiritual children.

gations that had sprung up in all of the great cities of the ancient world. Most of the converts to the new religion followed Paul's teachings and ignored the Jewish law. They devoted themselves wholeheartedly to their faith in Jesus.

The Christians, like the Jews from whom they had sprung, took seriously their moral standards and teachings, which were so different from those of the Romans. They encouraged equality among all men, as when slaves and freemen gathered to pray and share meals. No Christian would watch a gladiatorial contest in which men were killed for sport. Christians scoffed at the Romans' pride in their empire and in the great imperial armies. If a Roman boasted that he was off to the wars to defend Roman civilization against the barbarians, Christians would look at him and shake their heads in pity. For the Christians did not believe that any war could be just; they felt that the shedding of blood was wrong, even in capital punishment. After all, Jesus had told men to love their enemies, and fighting a war was a direct contradiction of this command.

But Christians had to be careful about stating their ideas aloud, even to a neighbor or a friend, for the government was suspicious of people who refused to serve in the

army and who scoffed at the glory of Rome. They looked on them as traitors or fools, or both. People like the Christians and the Jews were regarded with suspicion for their curious customs. Christians would not eat meat that was offered for sale in the cities, for instance. This was not because, like the Jews, they considered certain kinds of food taboo. It was customary to offer most animals to one pagan god or another as a gesture of piety when they were slaughtered for food, and the followers of Jesus would never eat meat left over from a pagan sacrifice.

The Christians would not even send their children to school, the way other people did. They did not want them to learn stories of the pagan gods and goddesses. They would not go to hospitals when they were sick, for they refused to place themselves under the care of the pagan god of healing, Aesculapius, to whom all hospitals were dedicated, as today a hospital might be dedicated to a particular saint. The women did not wear jewelry or use cosmetics, and they preferred to dress in clothing of subdued colors. If God had wanted women to wear clothes of purple wool, one of them said, then He would have made purple sheep.

Despite these difficult rules, thousands of people were converted to the new religion, risking the scorn of their neighbors and the persecution of the government. For, in an age that was notorious for wickedness and cruelty, the Christians maintained the highest standards of conduct, their legacy of morality from Judaism. They met reproach with charity, and persecution with bravery. Other people ignored or took advantage of the poor and the weak. The Christians helped them. Other people changed their ideas

The separation of early Christians from the pagan community was complete even in burial. Opposite is an apparently endless gallery of tombs in a third-century catacomb. A favorite theme of catacomb art was the Eucharist feast (right), a symbolic partaking of the body and blood of Jesus to show the belief in salvation and life eternal.

Many Christians suffered horrible deaths at the hands of their persecutors. The martyr at left appears in a twelfth-century fresco.

to conform to the latest fashion. Christians faithfully held to the same unchanging beliefs. Other people often felt cast adrift in the vast Roman world, powerless before the rich or rapacious government officials. Christians found a warm haven in their religion, and they demonstrated to the world the kindness and love that was a central theme of Christianity.

Most Romans failed to see the nobility of the new religion. Christians acquired a reputation of being atheists, for after all they did not worship the Roman gods. The eating of bread and the drinking of wine, symbolic of Jesus' body and blood, was derided as a form of ritual cannibalism. The Christians, moreover, were considered cowards because they would not fight. People began to complain to the authorities that Christians were traitors, for they would not worship the emperor. The imperial government, which soon came to agree with the persecutors of Christianity, offered to reward anyone who turned in a Christian for the crime of treason with the property of the accused.

When they were charged with treason, Christians claimed that they were not traitors. They were, they said, immune from the laws that ordered everybody except the Jews to worship the emperor. The Christians claimed that they too had the right to be exempt. In fact, they claimed that they—the Christians—were the true Jews, while the Jews themselves were heretics. For they believed that Christianity was the fulfillment of the Jewish religion, and the Jews, who failed to recognize this, were guilty of renouncing their heritage.

This complex reasoning failed to convince the Roman judges, however. "You have lived long years in the spirit of sacrilege," one of them declared to the leader of a Christian community in North Africa. "You have declared yourself the enemy of the gods of Rome and of its sacred laws."

One Roman governor named Pliny, who ruled a province in Asia Minor, was less sure that Christianity was a crime. He wrote a letter to the Emperor Trajan, around the year A.D. 111, asking him what to do with the Christians in his province.

"I have never been present at the trial of Christians," he wrote, "and I do not know what to ask or how to punish. I have been very much at a loss to know whether to make any distinction for age or strength, whether to excuse those who have renounced Christianity, whether the name itself, lacking other offense, or the crimes associated with the name should be punished. In the meantime, this is what I have done. I have asked the accused whether they were Christians. If they confessed, I asked a second and a third time, threatening penalty. Those who persisted I ordered to be executed, for I did not doubt that whatever it was they professed, they deserved to be punished for their inflexible obstinacy. There were others of equal madness, who because they were Roman citizens, I sent to Rome. Presently . . . more cases came to light. An anonymous document came in with many names. I dismissed those who said they were not or never had been Christians, and who in my presence supplicated the gods and placed wine and incense before your image, and especially cursed Christ, which I hear no true Christians will do."

The emperor answered Pliny that his handling of the Christians had been according to the law. If they were denounced, they were to be punished, but, for the time being, they were not to be hunted out. Later this policy was to change, and Christians were sought out and mercilessly slaughtered merely for believing in the new religion.

An early Christian wall-painting from the catacombs of Callistus depicts a child being baptized, a ritual symbolic of redemption.

When they faced execution, the Christians showed that they were by no means cowards, even though their death might be a horrible one—on the cross or thrown to the lions or killed by gladiators. Indeed, the bravery of the Christian martyrs was so great that even some of their persecutors were affected by it. Many Romans were converted to the new religion, which could bring such faith and strength to the hearts of ordinary people. For the martyrs often faced the prospect of death with calmness and even with joy because they believed that death at the hands of their persecutors meant that their souls would be saved to enter heaven. They believed that the earth, which would soon be destroyed, held no glory for them; only heaven did. For they expected that Jesus would return and end the world, judging the living and the dead and sending them to heaven or to hell.

Rome was persecuting them, but Rome, they believed, was almost at the end of its history. They thought that the Roman Empire was the work of the Devil and that soon the Devil would be overthrown while the followers of Jesus sat in glory in heaven.

While Jewish scholars were devoting their efforts to interpreting the laws of the Torah, Christian scholars were engaged in a similar intellectual endeavor, pondering various interpretations of the life of Jesus. It took many years to arrive at an explanation of the relationship between Jesus and God, and there were many arguments about it. But by the second century after Jesus' death, most Christians had come to believe that he was God made man and that he had descended to earth from heaven and sacrificed himself so that men, after death, could go from earth to heaven. For Christians believed that men were basically sinful, and only through God's great mercy, which was shown in Jesus' coming to earth, could they ever be saved.

These ideas appear in several books that were written during the first and second centuries A.D. and which go to make up the New Testament. Christians added these works to the Jewish Bible and came to revere them as the basic account of their faith. The first four books, the Gospels of Matthew, Mark, Luke, and John, which tell the story of Jesus' life, show the evolution of ideas about Jesus, for they were written in different times and places. The fifth book, the Acts of the Apostles, narrates the early history of the Christian church in Jerusalem and recounts the missionary activities of Peter and Paul. The Epistles, written by Paul and other church leaders, also show how varied were the beliefs about Jesus and Christianity that prevailed in churches in different cities or even within individual congregations. The authors of the Epistles attempt to resolve these differences. The last book of the New Testament, the Revelation to John, describes the end of the world and Jesus' return to save the faithful Christians and punish the wicked Romans. Taken together, the New Testament sets forth the basic beliefs of the Christian faith. It was through reading these books that many converts were first attracted to Christianity and were able to maintain their faith despite the cruelest persecution.

Around the year A.D. 112, according to tradition, Christians in the city of Rome were startled by a rumor. The Emperor Trajan, it was said, was eager to have the support of the Jews for a campaign he was planning against the Persians and was going to rebuild the Temple of Jerusalem. The emperor had decided that the Jews had been punished enough for their rebellion fifty years earlier. Judaea, in this period, had indeed grown prosperous, and the Jews had already regained many of their former rights. Now they were going to be permitted to return to Jerusalem and re-establish the Temple there.

Many Christians were worried and angry when they heard this. They believed that God had destroyed Jerusalem and the Temple to punish the Jews for ignoring Jesus; that the destruction of the Temple proved that the old way of doing things, the observance of the Jewish law and the sacrifice of animals, was meaningless; and that the sacrifice of Jesus on the cross marked the beginning of a new religion. If the Temple were rebuilt it might mean that the Jews were right after all and that Jesus was not the Messiah.

The Jews, on the other hand, were overjoyed. But in the midst of their celebrations, arguments broke out about the rebuilding of the Temple. The Christians were not the only ones who opposed its reconstruction. Even some Jews—nationalists who wanted to fight the war with Rome all over again and re-establish Jewish independence—were against it. They thought it should be rebuilt by Jews and not by Romans. The Samaritans, who hated the Jews, also opposed the rebuilding. Finally, it became evident that the Temple was not going to be rebuilt after all.

A few years later, relations between the Romans and the Jews again took a turn for the worse. In 115, rebellions broke out against the Romans in Egypt, North Africa, and Cyprus, where there were large communities of Jews, but they were harshly suppressed. In the following decade,

A beneficent and unpretentious Roman emperor, Trajan ruled in the early years of the second century.

OSTIA MUSEUM: LEONARD VON MATT

Jews were once more subjected to rigorous laws, to make sure that they would not rebel again. They were forbidden to practice certain rites of their religion that seemed to encourage Jewish nationalism. For instance, it was forbidden to sound the *shofar*—the ram's horn—during some religious ceremonies because it seemed to the Romans like a military trumpet calling the Jews to rebel. This was despite the fact that the ram's horn had been sounded in Jewish religious ceremonies for more than a thousand years. Prayers proclaiming the Jewish God as the only deity were also banned. In addition, Jewish judges were deprived of the right to grant divorces, and no Jewish child was allowed to be circumcised.

The Jewish underground organized for another battle against Rome. Once again the Jews expected the Messiah to come and deliver them, ushering in the kingdom of God.

In the midst of the Jews' preparations, the Romans announced that they were going to rebuild Jerusalem and its Temple after all. The Emperor Trajan's successor, Hadrian, visited Judaea during a tour of the Middle East in the years 130 and 131. It had been a mistake to destroy Jerusalem, he decided; the city was too famous and too beautiful to lie in ruins. Moreover, its site was too strategic to remain unoccupied. Hadrian would rebuild it, he announced, but as a Roman city. The temple to be erected there would be dedicated not to the God of the Jews but to the emperor himself as the personification of Jupiter.

When this news spread through the Judaean countryside, a new rebellion broke out. Under the leadership of a man named Simon bar-Kochba, the Jews gathered at the ruins of the city of Jerusalem and vowed to fight once more until death to drive the Romans out of the country.

At first the hastily organized and badly armed rebels won a few victories. The Jews were thrilled with their successes. Rumors began to sweep through the nation that the Messiah had come and that the Roman power was finally going to be overthrown. Bar-Kochba, a wise and skillful military leader, was hailed as the Messiah. His followers interpreted his name to mean "Son of the Star," an epithet of the Messiah. But he was reluctant to claim Messiahship or to use that title; so he called himself prince of Israel.

A photograph of present-day Jerusalem focuses on the old city, now in the kingdom of Jordan. The Dome of the Rock (left, middleground) is on the site of the ancient Temple. In the background is Israel and the new city.

He was not to be prince of Israel very long. For two and a half years he and his followers managed to control Jerusalem and most of Judaea as well. The priesthood was reinstated, and sacrifices were once more offered on the Temple site. The nation of Israel, it seemed, had been reborn. But Rome was still master of the world. In the year A.D. 134 Jerusalem fell once again. Bar-Kochba and his men fled southward into the wilderness forts of Judaea, just as the Zealots had fled after the fall of Jerusalem in the year A.D. 70. The rebels held out one year longer; but in the summer of 135, their last fortress, Beitar, was finally captured. The prince of Israel was killed, and the second rebellion of the Jews was, to all practical purposes, at an end.

Half a million people were slain in this revolt, which rivaled in size and brutality the one ended in the year 70. Thousands of Jews were sold into slavery. Hundreds of their villages were wiped out, their houses burned, their trees cut down. All the descendants of King David who might claim to be the Messiah were hunted down and slaughtered by the Romans. Judaea was virtually deserted; even the birds, it was said, avoided the country, for there was nothing to support them there. Jerusalem was rebuilt by the Romans, and so that the Jewish name would be forgotten, it was renamed Aelia Capitolina. A pagan temple was built there, and the figure of a swine, an animal considered unclean by the Jews, was carved over the gate. No Jew was allowed to enter the city; any Jew caught inside would be put to death. Even the name of the province was changed, for Judaea was a Jewish name. From then on the region was to be known as Palestina, after the Philistines who had once lived in one part of it.

But far worse than all of the changes of name, and worse than the destruction of the countryside, was the edict that outlawed the Jewish religion. No Jew was to be allowed to worship God any more. The observance of the laws of the Bible was forbidden. And the study and teaching of the law were forbidden too.

Many Jews fled to Babylonia, where they could live under Persian rule and practice their religion freely. And so, through death and exile the Jewish population of the Holy Land decreased until it was only a fraction of what it had been a century or two earlier. In the little town of Usha in Galilee, the rabbis in assembly decided that the entire Jewish people would have to go into hiding. Although no one wanted to lie to deny his religion, they decided that it was all right to hide the fact that one was a Jew if it meant

Emperor Hadrian, a great soldier and builder, was the last ruler to extend the imperial boundaries.

saving one's life. Nevertheless, there were still three sins that the pagans could never force a Jew to commit: murder, unchastity, and the worship of idols.

In these decades, the Romans tortured and killed many martyrs, for according to their edicts, both Judaism and Christianity were illegal. Rome offered to Christians and Jews the chance to recant. If they promised to worship idols, they could go free, be honored by their neighbors, respected by the authorities, and enjoy the peaceful life of the Roman citizen. The Romans were powerful, and the Jews and the Christians were pitifully weak. There seemed no reason to the Romans why these minorities should not stop suffering and join the victorious majority to enjoy the benefits of power. But both the Jews and the Christians had something that the Romans could not understand, a religious faith that was more important to them than peace or money or safety or even life itself. And it was this faith that enabled them to outlast their oppressors.

Whenever there was need for a scapegoat, Christians and Jews suffered persecution. "If the Tiber floods or the Nile fails to flood, if the skies darken, if the earth trembles, if famine, war, or plague occurs, then immediately the shout goes up: 'The Christians to the lion!'"—a second-century Christian writer complained. He was right. At the slightest provocation, the Christians were tortured and killed because they were different. And long after the Christians had become the majority, for century after century, the Jews were persecuted even more, and by Christians too.

But it was not the powerful Romans who were to survive. It was the weak—the Christians and the Jews—who managed to overcome horrifying persecution and to flourish for thousands of years, long after the Roman Empire had crumbled.

In the city of the Caesars there are now hundreds of churches that have risen, dedicated to the faith of Jesus, who was killed because he was accused of plotting against Caesar's rule. And a cross stands in the ruins of the Colosseum, where hundreds of Christians met a martyr's death. The Roman Empire is gone, but the Jews, since the establishment of the state of Israel in 1948, have their own independent nation again. And in the ruined Roman Forum, on the Arch of Titus, which shows the victorious Romans marching with plunder from the defeated city of Jerusalem, a few Hebrew words can be seen, scratched with a stone by a tourist, come from the Holy Land to visit Rome. "*Am Yisroel chai*," it reads, "The people of Israel live."

A shekel struck by bar-Kochba in A.D. 135, during the abortive second Jewish revolt, is decorated with a likeness of Herod's Temple.

NATIONAL MUSEUM, SARAJEVO: COURTESY FRANK J. DARMSTAEDTER, JEWISH THEOLOGICAL SEMINARY OF AMERICA

A thirteenth-century Spanish Haggada illumination depicts the Passover seder.

AMERICAN HERITAGE
PUBLISHING CO., INC.

James Parton, *President*
Richard M. Ketchum, *Editorial Director, Book Division*
Stephen W. Sears, *Editor, Education Department*
Irwin Glusker, *Art Director*

HORIZON CARAVEL BOOKS

JOSEPH L. GARDNER, *Managing Editor*
Janet Czarnetzki, *Art Director*
Elaine K. Andrews, *Copy Editor*
Mary Leverty, *Picture Researcher*
Nancy Simon, *Editorial Researcher*
Jessica R. Baerwald, *Editorial Assistant*
Gertrudis Feliu, *Chief, European Bureau*
Claire de Forbin, *European Bureau*

ACKNOWLEDGMENTS

The Editors are indebted to the following individuals and institutions for their generous assistance in preparing this book:

Bibliothèque Nationale, Paris
British Museum, London—M. A. McKenzie
Brooklyn Museum, Department of Ancient Art—Donaldson F. Hoopes
Frank J. Darmstaedter, Jewish Theological Seminary of America, New York
Ronald Harker, London
Hebrew Union College, Cincinnati, Ohio—Dr. Joseph Gutmann, Mrs. Minnie Levine
Judith Herschlag, B'nai Brith, New York
Mrs. Mary Jenkins, London
Kunsthistorisches Museum, Vienna—Dr. Edwin M. Auer
National Gallery of Art, Washington, D.C.—Mrs. Ruth Dundas
Smithsonian Institution, Freer Gallery of Art, Washington, D.C.—Harold P. Stern
Bianca Spantigati, Rome
Mrs. Maria Todorow, Florence
University of Michigan Photographic Services, Ann Arbor—Fred Anderegg

FURTHER READING

Adler, Morris, *The World of the Talmud*. Schocken Books, 1963.

Bainton, Roland H., *The Horizon Book of Christianity*. American Heritage Publishing Co., Inc., 1964.

Bergeaud, Jean, *John The Baptist*, trans. by Jane Saul, R. S. C. J. The Macmillan Company, 1962.

Bokser, Rabbi Ben Zion, *The Wisdom of the Talmud*. The Citadel Press, 1962.

Coss, Thurman L., *Secrets from the Caves; A Layman's Guide to the Dead Sea Scrolls*. Abingdon Press, 1963.

Daniel-Rops, Henri, *Daily Life in the Time of Jesus*. Mentor-Omega Book, 1964.

————*The Church of Apostles and Martyrs*, 2 vols. Doubleday Image Book, 1962.

Daniel to Paul, Gaalyahu Cornfeld, ed. The Macmillan Company, 1962.

Dictionary of the Bible, rev. ed., Frederick C. Grant and H. H. Rowley, eds. Charles Scribner's Sons, 1963.

Davies, A. Powell, *The First Christian: A Study of St. Paul and Christian Origins*. Mentor, 1959.

Finkelstein, Louis, *Akiba*. Meridian Books and The Jewish Publication Society, 1962.

————*The Pharisees*, 2 vols., rev. ed. The Jewish Publication Society, 1961.

Goguel, Maurice, *Jesus and the Origins of Christianity*, 2 vols. Harper Torchbooks, 1960.

Herford, R. Travers, *The Pharisees*. Beacon Press, 1962.

Josephus, Flavius, *Complete Works*. Kregel Publications, 1960.

Klausner, Joseph, *Jesus of Nazareth: His Life, Times, and Teaching*. Beacon Press, 1964.

Lietzmann, Hans, *A History of the Early Church*, 2 vols. Meridian Books, 1961.

Noth, Martin, *The History of Israel*, rev. ed. Harper & Brothers, 1960.

Oxford Bible Atlas, Herbert G. May, ed. Oxford University Press, 1960.

Paine, Robert, *The Horizon Book of Ancient Rome*. American Heritage Publishing Co., Inc., 1966.

Perowne, Stewart, *The Life and Times of Herod the Great*. Arrow Books, 1960.

Pfeiffer, R. H., *History of New Testament Times*. Harper & Brothers, 1949.

Sachar, Abram Leon, *A History of the Jews*. Alfred A. Knopf, 1965.

Schürer, Emil, *A History of the Jewish People in the Time of Jesus*. Schocken Books, 1961.

The Zondervan Pictorial Bible Dictionary, Merrill C. Tenney, ed. Zondervan Publishing House, 1963.

INDEX

Bold face indicates pages on which maps or illustrations appear

Aaron, **front endsheet,** 8
Abraham, 33, 36, **98, 99**
Acts of the Apostles, 83, 87, 88, 104, 144
Aesculapius, 141
Ananias, 88
Andrew, 59, 63, **63**
Antigonus, 17, 19, 22, 25
Antioch, 90, 92, 93, 96
Antipater, 16
Antiquities of the Jews, 125
    illustrated manuscript from, **11, 24, 125**
Antonia fortress, 29, **29,** 101, 127
Antony, Marc, 14, 16, 17, **17,** 21, 127
Apostles, 62, **62,** 65, **65,** 83, **83,** 107
Arabia, 14, 35
Ark of the Covenant, 30, **30,** 32
Asia Minor, 85, 93, 96, 143
Assyrians, 34, 129
Athanasius of Alexandria, Bishop, 108
Athens, 11, 96, 98
Augustus, Emperor, 40
Babylonia, 138, 148
    temples of, 31
Babylonians, 26, 34, 37, 129, 135
Baptism, 49, 50, **143**
Beatitudes, 65
Beitar, 148
Beth Alpha synagogue, 32
    mosaic from, **32**
Bethlehem, 52, 58, 133
Bethsaida, 58
Bible, 12, 38, 77, 80, 124, 135, 138, 148
Book of Deuteronomy, 36
Book of Exodus, 36
Book of Genesis, 36
Book of Joshua, 36
Book of Judges, 36
Book of Kings, 36
Book of Leviticus, 36
Book of Numbers, 36
Book of Revelation, 108
Book of Samuel, 36
Caesarea, 52, 95, **100,** 101, 114
Callistus, catacomb of, 143
    wall painting from, **143**
Cana, feast in, 59, **59**
Capernaum, 57
Capitoline Hill, 21
Carthage, 11
Chartres Cathedral, 60
    stained glass window from, **60**
Christian churches, 138, 149
Christianity, 14, 49, 83, 88, 92, 98, 101, 108, 111, 142, 145
    converts to, 138–141 *passim,* 144
    Judaism and, 62, 95, 143, 149
Christians, 92, 101, 102, 107, 117, 139, 145
    faith of, 139–142, 144, 145, 149
    gentile, 92
    Jewish, 92, 95
    persecution of, 142–144, **142**
    teachings of, 39

Coptic illuminations, **cover,** 8, 56, **56,** 108, **109**
Corinth, 96
    ruins of, **96–97**
Crete, 102
Cyprus, 96, 145
Damascus, 12, 84, 87, 88, 90, **90,** 91
Daniel in the lion's den, 38, **38**
David, King, 8, **8,** 34, 54, **54,** 58, 148
Day of Judgment, 50, 52
Dead Sea, 12, 19, 23, 43, 47, 49, 53, 54, 134
Dead Sea Scrolls, 44, **44, 45,** 47
Demeter, 98, 99
Diaspora, the, 35, 85
Dome of the Rock, 146, **146**
Duccio, 74, 83
    altarpiece by, **82**
    painting by, **74–75**
Dura-Europos, synagogue, 8, 30, 36
    frescoes, **front endsheet, 30, 36–37**
Egypt, 11, 21, 34, 35, 98, 145
Egyptian gods, 31
Egyptians, 36, **36–37,** 129
Eleazar, 133
Eleusis, 98–99
Elijah, 57, 58, 65, **65**
Epistles, 144–145
    See also Paul
Essenes, 43–50 *passim,* 52, 54, 55, 117, 138
    scriptorium of, 47
Eucharist, 141, **141**
Ephesus, 96
Evangelists, the Four, 108, **108, 109**
Ezekiel, 36, 108
Felix, Roman procurator, 101
Festus, Roman procurator, 102, 111
Florus, Roman procurator, 114
Fouquet, Jean, 11, 24, 125
    illuminations by, **10, 24, 125**
Franciscan Church of All Nations, 72, **72–73**
Galilee, 12, 16, 19, 22, 59, 65, 69, 117, 138, 148
    countryside of, **23, 115**
Gamaliel, rabbis, 85, 87, 124, 136, **136,** 137
Gebel Musa range, 35
    north peak of, **35**
Gemara, 138
Gentiles, 91, 92, 111
Gethsemane, 70, 72, **72–73,** 74, **74–75**
Giotto, 60, 70
    Last Supper fresco by, **70–71**
    Nativity scene by, **60–61**
Golgotha, 77, 78, **78–79,** 80, 81, 118
Gospel According to John, 58, 68, 70, 108, 144
Gospel According to Luke, 58, 59, 60, 108, 144
Gospel According to Mark, 58, 107, 108, 144
Gospel According to Matthew, 58, 59, 108, 144
Gospels, 58, 60, 69, 72, 77, 83, 108, 144
Greece, 11, 35, 93, 96
Greek culture, 14, 40
Greeks, 38, 91, 129
Hadrian, Emperor, 146, 148, **148**

Haggada, 33, 36, 136, 150
    illuminations from, **36, 136, 150**
    See also Yaffe, Meir
Hammam Lif, synagogue at, 46
    mosaic panels from, **46, 47**
Hasmonaeans, 16, 19, 38, 43, 46
Hebrews, 34
Hebrew tribes, 26, 31, 33
Herod, King, 14, 16, 17, 19, 24, **24,** 26, 28, 33, 38–41 *passim,* 43, 46, 47, 72, 114, 127, 133, 134
    palace of, **18,** 19
    named King of the Jews, 21–22
    assaults Jerusalem, 23–25
    death of, 49, 52–53
Herod Antipas, Tetrarch of Galilee, 53, **53,** 54, **54,** 55, 57, 58, 60, 65, 69
Herodias, 54, 55
Herodium, 133
Hillel, Rabbi, 39, 137
Hyrcanus, 16, 17
Idumaea, 12, 16
Idumaeans, 12
Isaiah, 36, 37, 46, 50
Israel, 32, 34, 44, 146, 148, 149
    Twelve Tribes of, 34
Israelites, 33, 34, 37, 46, 49
Israelite slaves, 26, **27**
James, 92
Jeremiah, 36
Jerusalem, 6, **7,** 16, 17, 19, 22–28 *passim,* 30, 31, 34, 40, 41, 46, 50, 52, 65, 66, **66–67,** 69–72 *passim,* **72–73,** 78, 80, 85, **86,** 87, 88, 91–95 *passim,* 101, 111–129 *passim,* 136, 137, 146, **146–147,** 149
    houses of, **112–113**
    rebellion in, 114–115
    Jewish defense of, 119–129 *passim*
    fall of, 132, 133, 138
    rebuilt by Romans, 148
Jericho, 23
Jesse, 8, **8**
Jesus, **7, 8, 62, 63, 64, 68, 69, 70, 77, 80, 84, 108, back endsheet,** 6, 8, 12, 49, 57–95 *passim,* 107, 108, 114, 118, 137, 138, 139, 141, 149
    family tree of, **8**
    birth of, 56, 60, **60–61**
    baptism of, 56, **56–57,** 58
    teachings of, 59, 62
    miracles of, 58–59, **58, 59**
    Transfiguration of, **65**
    Disciples of, 49, 58, 59, 62, 70, **70,** 74, **74–75,** 78, **78,** 81, 83, 92
    followers of, 59, 62, 65, 80, **80,** 91, 92, 141, 144
    arrest of, **74–75,** 76
    trial of, 72–73, 77
    Crucifixion of, **78–79,** 80–81, 83, 85, 98
    Resurrection of, **82,** 83, **83,** 95, 99, 104
    Ascension of, 83, **83**
    as the Messiah, 57, 65, 69, 72, 73, 83, 87, 91, 95, 98, **98–99,** 117, 145
    as the Good Shepherd, **139**
Jewish religion, *See* Judaism
Jewish War, The, 132
    illumination from, **132–133**
Jews, 12, 14, 16, 17, 21–43 *passim,* 59, 65, 68, 70, 72, 77, 80, 85, 91, 92, 95, 96, 101, 104, 111–116

passim, 118, 137, 139, 141, 143, 145, 146
faith of, 22, 32–41 *passim*, 46, 49, 50, 52, 135, 149
defeated by King Herod, **24,** 25–28 *passim*
dispersion of, 33–35
defend Jerusalem, 119–128 *passim*
defeated by Romans, 129–135
Jochanan ben Zakkai, 124–127, 129, 135, 137
John the Baptist, 8, 48–55, *passim*, **48, 50,** 58, 59, 85, 114, 133, **back endsheet**
baptism of Jesus, 56, **56–57**
beheaded, **54,** 55, 57
John the Evangelist, **cover,** 8, 78, **78–79,** 81, 108, **109**
Jordan River, 34, 49, 50, **51,** 53, 54, 56, 57, 58, 62, 69
Joseph ben Caiaphas, 70
Joseph of Arimathea, 81
Josephus, 119, 125, 132, **133,** 134
Judaea, 12, 14, 16, 17, 19, 22, 26, 39, 59, 88, 129, 133, 145, 146, 148
Judah, 34
lion of, 26, **26, 32**
Judah ha-Nasi, Rabbi, 138
Judaic Code, 92
Judaism, 12, 14, 62, 85, 92, 129, 135, 138, 141, 148, 149
Christianity and, 62, 95, 143, 149
Judas, 70, **70, 74,** 75, 76, **76**
Jupiter, 146
Temple of, 21
Last Supper, 49, **70–71,** 92, 98, 107
Lazarus, raising of, 59, **59**
Luke, **cover,** 8, 59, 108, **109**
Maccabee, Judas, 38
Maccabees, the, 39
battle with Seleucidae, **39**
Macedonia, 96
Machaerus, fort of, 54, 55, 133
dungeon of, 57
Madeba basilica, 112–113
mosaic map from, **112–113**
Malta, 102
Mantegna, Andrea, 78
painting by, **78–79**
Maps
Jerusalem in A.D. 70, **118**
Old and New Testament sites, **13**
Paul's Missionary Journeys, **93**
Marcus Aurelius, Column of, **110,** 111, 116, **116, 117**
Mark, **cover,** 8, 107, 108, **109**
Mary, 8, **8,** 58, 60, **60–61,** 78, **78, back endsheet**
Joseph and, 60, **60–61**
Mary Magdalene, 83
Masada, fort of, 19, 21, 43, 114, 133, 134, 135
ruins of, 134, **134**
site of, **18**
Massacre of the Innocents, 52, **52**
Matthew, **cover,** 8, 108, **109**
Mediterranean Sea, 11, 12, 113, 119
Mediterranean world, 11, 12, 14, 17, 93, 111
Menorahs, 32, **32**
Mesopotamia, 33
Messiah, 43, 46, 47, 49, 50, 52, 54, 57, 58, 59, 62, 107, 124, 146, 148

Micah, 36, 37, 50
Mishnah, 138
Moses, 26, **27,** 34, 35, 36, **36,** 46, 54, **54,** 98–99
law of, 50, 52, 98
leading the Exodus, **36–37**
Mount of Olives, 70, 72, **72–73,** 111, 114
Mount Sinai, 34, 35, **35**
Mount Scopus, 118, 119
Mount Tabor, 65
Nathan, 50
Nazarenes, 87, 90, 92
Nero, Emperor, 104, 107, **107**
New Testament, 58, 60, 81, 88, 96, 107, 108, 145
Octavian, 14, 16, **16,** 17, **17**
Old Testament, 36, 38, 58, 99, 108
Palestine, 12, 14, 16, 19, 22, 28, 33–38 *passim*, 43, 47, 50, 52, 69, 96, 101, 107, 111, 112, 134, 138
Palestine Archaeological Museum, 44
Parthians, 17, 19
Passover, 33, 69, 70, 72, 77, 137, 150
Passover seder, **150**
Paul, 84, **84,** 88–111 *passim*, **91, 95, 99, 103, 105,** 124, 139, 144
Apostle to Gentiles, 95
Epistles of, 93, **93,** 96, 99–101, 107
death of, **106**
See also Saul of Tarsus
Pella, 117
Peraea, 69
Peter, 87, 92, 98, **99,** 106, 107, 108, 144
Apostle to the Jews, 95
death of, **106**
See also Simon Peter
Petra, 14, **14,** 21
treasury facade of, **13,** 14
Pharisees, 39–41, 43, 50, 52, 59, 65, 68, 72, 85, 87, 115, 135, 138
Phasael, 16, 19
Philistines, 148
Pliny, 143
Pompey the Great, 12, **12**
troops of, **10,** 11
Pontius Pilate, 69, 70, 76, **76,** 77, 80, 99, **99**
Psalter of Saint Louis, 26
illustration from, **27**
Qumran, **42,** 43, 44, 47, 49, 117
Ravenna, mosaic from, 63, **63**
Revelation to John, 145
Roman army, cavalrymen, 116, **116**
guards, 78, **79**
legionaries, **11,** 25, **110,** 111, 116, **117,** 122, **122,** 127, 128, **128**
soldiers, 77, **77,** 80, 111
troops, 22, 101, 114, 117, **130–131,** 131, 133
Roman Empire, 14, 88, 91, 101, 132, 134, 144, 149
Roman Forum, **20–21,** 21, 132, 149
Roman rule, 11–12, 40, 46, 52, 55, 85
Romans, 14, 16, 17, 19, 26, 46, 47, 62, 65, 70, 77, 80, 81, 91, 104, 107, 111, 114–134 *passim*, 138, 139, 142, 144, 145–146, 148, 149
Rome, 11, 12, 14, 17, 22, 35, 49, 65, 70, 72, 73, 85, 93, 98, 102, 104, 107, 108, 111, 129, 132, 144, 148

Rossano Gospels, 68, 70, 76
illustrations from, **68, 70, 76**
Sadducees, 40–41, 43, 59, 65, 68, 69, 70, 72, 138
Salome, 53, **53,** 54, **54,** 55
Samaria, 12, 19
Samaritans, 12, 34, 145
Sanhedrin, 17, 72, 73, 87, 101, 137
tombs of, 81, **81**
Saturn, Temple of, 21
remains of, **20–21**
Saul of Tarsus, 85–90
See also Paul
Sea of Galilee, 57, 58, **62,** 63, **63,** 88, 115, **115,** 117
Sebaste, 52
Sermon on the Mount, 62, **64,** 65
Shammai, Rabbi, 137
Shechem, 34
Shemaiah, 17
Shrine of the Book, 44, **44–45**
Sicarii, 111, 117
Simon bar-Kochba, 146–148, 149
Simon of Cyrene, 80
Simon Peter, 59, 63, **63,** 70, 74, **74**
Solomon, King, 26, 34, 38
Temple of, 26
Stephen, 87, 88, **88**
Synoptic Gospels, 108
Syria, 16, 17
Talmud, 138
Temple in Jerusalem, **10,** 11, 26–32 *passim,* **29,** 37, 38, 39, 43, 50, 65, 68, **68,** 69, 72, 80, 101, 115, 117, 118, **118,** 119, 124–127 *passim,* **125,** 135, 137, 138, 145
completion of, 114
Court of the Gentiles, 28, 29, **29**
Holy of Holies, 28, 30, 128
Romans forbid reconstruction of, 132
sacrifices in, 28, 31–32, 39, 46, 118, 128, 148
destruction of, 128–129, 135, 137
Ten Commandments, 8, 34, 50, 137, **back cover**
Thanksgiving Psalms, 44, **44**
Thessalonica, 96
Theudas, 62–65, 114
Tiber River, 107, 149
Tiberius, Emperor, 57
Titus, 118, 119, **119,** 128, 129, 132, **132**
Arch of, **130–131,** 131, 132, 149
besieges Jerusalem, 119, 123
Torah, 12, 36, 38, 39, 50, 59, 85, 87, 124, 135, 137, 138, 144
Trajan, Emperor, 143, 145, **145,** 146
Column of, 122, **122**
Vatican Hill, 107
Veneziano, Domenico, 48
painting by, **48–49**
Vespasian, Emperor, 129, 132, **132**
Vesta, altar of, 22
relief from, **22**
Via Dolorosa, 77, **77**
Yaffe, Meir, 33, 34, 127, 137
Haggada illustrations by, **33, 34, 127, 137**
Yahweh, 31
Yavneh, 126, 129, 135, 136, 137, 138
Zealots, 40, 115, 117, 118, 133, 134, 148